T

AMERIKA

Book II

AN ANDREW JACKSON

A History and Play

For the Theatre of the Mind

By

Joseph Eldredge

Annotated, with a forward by the author

CHOICE
PUBLICATIONS

Cover art and design by Baris Sehri
Set in Times New Roman font
Printed in the United States of America

ISBN 979-8-9900751-4-6

For gods and country...

CONTENTS

FORWARD

An Andrew Jackson is an uncanny book, one that tells the history of our seventh President, in a manner which is both lyrical and visionary.

Attempt has been made, on the part of the poet, to craft, with broadest of license, a Song of our President's life, especially as it correlated to the 'growing up' of our own young Country. The style of this story, however, is archaic, strange, even primitive, in its syntax, imagery, and theme – as is much of the world's ancient literature. Does he seem ancient to *US*?

Quickly then does our idea of *America* change...

What we must tell of ancient Andrew Jackson, and what we must not, speaks to the enormous Power with which enormous historical figures affect us. To expiate our ills, it is necessary to pose them, no matter their sordidity, whether historically or poetically. Like with any dream, to bring to consciousness (through the music of thought, which is poetry) is to cull the adversity of the repressed.

I present him to you. Listen. Tread carefully on him.

AN ANDREW JACKSON

ACT 1

SOUTH CAROLINA TERRITORY –
SPRING 1767

Listen, an Andrew Jackson, down from the lowlands of the East, rose to settle in the pines above Twelve Tally Creek. Everywhere there, rich red clay, towering black forest, a wilderness. Himself he carried the broad logs away. Himself toiled his land. There was clearing, planting. From the sweat of his face, a log cabin raised. His wife, his two sons, warm in there. Head of his family, so a third went in the womb.

*This Andrew Jackson was a son of England. Crowns sat on his mantle – coin heads. One day – he was felling the pines – he did not hear– a push – "Timber!" – a pine fell on his crown and cracked it in. And this Andrew Jackson, everywhere, lay a rich red clay. His bier goes bodiless to burial. His initial'd pine-box is brought to the plot: **A.J.** came to term.*

SOUTH CAROLINA TERRITORY –
JULY 4TH, 1776 – THE FIRST VISION

An Andrew Jackson had begot an Andrew Jackson. Andrew was a lifefull boy. He loved to attend to the church; he sang

9

there the loudest. He loved to wrestle, and often lost his bouts. He was very tall. He was very thin. He loved to laugh. He loved to shoot, to shout, to shove, falling over with the blast of the gunvalve, whips any boy that laughs at him on the ground. He laughs at himself on the ground. He laughs, himself shaping the palette'd clouds, 'It is an old man with a billowing beard', 'It is a horses heads', 'It is a brown Bess.'

This Andrew Jackson was walking through the spiring pines where he found a stone well, covering itself with bramble and with brake. Andrew broke it away. Down deep he looked: a shallow pool, clear water there, a reflection there or, the body of a boy, sprawled on his back like a star gazing back. Andrew, suspended, might've frozen in stupor, had not the boy at the bottom of the well stirred the pool and said:

ANDREW

BOY IN WELL

Halloo.

ANDREW

Halloo! I thought you were my face.

BOY IN WELL

I am fearfully sorry about that.

ANDREW

That's ok. Why are you lying down there anyway?

BOY IN WELL

I can't recall. Perhaps I fell backwards.

Or perhaps by a push was that slip down.

Maybe, either, long I lay in the well,

Eyes sealed to the scrolls of the rolling Time

Till not a memory remained to mine,

All was dark, always so, to till me new sight

I woke, eyes wide: a star spangled night,

Starry and glare to my boundaries' scope,

Vision imbued me until,

My memory of myself foregone,

I reckon'd those stars fathers and mothers,

Those planets sisters and brothers, bannered

By all cosmos surmised I my descent,

So made myself to their forms the mimic,

In hopes they'd see me from this spot, carry

Me up to firmament without a thought,

But I lay long in the well, too long in

The well, so old as abyss' ancient[1] I

Immobile, distant as those deep's beacons,

Became immobile myself, distant be

Myself, an indifferent self, cycloptic round

This tunnel being only one eye, and

This well being only body, earth hemmed,

Tower'd downward, a seeing ruin,

---

[1] a flag bearer

I'd forgot I was a boy and became

A well, well, 'til you, vision to Vision saw me!

In eyes' reflect, fires vital'r than all stars,

A shock of sight to life, spur to burning,

A billows phram'd to breath into this nose,

As furnaces leapt up, words to the tongue,

Words on tongues, coals carried with tongs,

Inflamed, I recalled, Speech was me,

And that I'll Tongue in you.

ANDREW

Well… Do you think you can come up and out?

Fiery, leaping vault! He stands on the sill of the well his hands on his hips his legs spread his grin wide with his boyish smile stretching out to the very corners.

ANDREW
(*amazed*)

What is your name???

SAHM

I am SAHM all in all.

Andrew sat down on the ground SAHM sat down on the wall of the well. He regarded aground all the forest, Andrew followed his gaze around. Look, their eyes, they meet, living there together.

SAHM

Listen, I've said of something wonderful.

ANDREW

(laughing)

Haha! What is it? I'm listening, Sam!

SAHM

(raising his arms, a motion)

This my unanimous declaration!

Throw off the old garments! I have raiment

In abundance for you! I gab to garb

The new Man! The new Man is of himself

A People, apart from ancients, and with Self

An equal. He shall have one name, without

An end shall be his fame, shall be no veil

Before his eyes, man walking ahead, behind,

All Truths he held self-evident of him,

His Rights he employ'd in power, ever

Unto his Life without a wall an edge,

He shall leap bounding with wild Liberty,

His tongue shall pant in pursuit of Happiness!

In an Independent Hall in Pennsylvania stately men stand to surround to spit word a hornéd King hosted in their midst. They sling their words like stones at the King in their midst.

13

THE FOUNDING FATHERS
(staccato)

He has refused his assent to Law!

He has dissolved the manly Houses!

He has refused the raise of the Elect!

He has prevented the population!

He has raised his stretched armies against us!

The seas, they overturn. The towns, they burn.

The coasts, ravage. Births thrown out in water.

He brings in Indians from the edges. The pointed

Arrow the sharp knife, over their shoulders our kin

Are slung in scalps!

The King is a goat. SAHM stands in mid, heads taller than the tallest, pale & horn & craning. His ring of men hem in, hem in.

The cracking of a gun into a crowd in Boston. The trading, in the marketplace, of blows for blows for – for bloody cobblestones.

SAHM
(wild with vision; bounding through the breasted pines)

Shall all a man be an Amerikan!

And his states of mort[1] and birth, of joy and

---

[1] death

14

Of dispair[1], shall not be afear'd of him,

For in one place I do Unite such States!

He runs out of earshot. Andrew lies on the ground, as though thrown from a firing gun. His head bleeds. He's lain like a star. He pants. He feels with his hand the humming of his throat, the soreness of his tongue.

THE FAMILY CABIN – EVENING

Elizabeth keeps the house. She changes the beds, sweeps the floors, holds open doors, ushers night and companions day. She raises her three sons: Hugh and Robert and Andrew the youngest. Andrew watches, his head on his hands, as she fashions a rocking chair, sits and sways there, knits a quilt, spreads warmth with the quilt, hums a song. Enter, Robert:

ROBERT JACKSON
(*singing*)

'The Elfin knight stands on yon hill[2],

Blaw, blaw, blaw winds, blaw

Blawing his horn loud and shrill.

And the wind has blawin my plaid awa'

---

[1] an un-unity

[2] "The Elfin Knight" - traditional Scottish folk ballad

Robert roves circumferentially the one-room cabin, as Elizabeth conducts him with her sowing needle, humming.

ANDREW JACKSON

Play on the song…

ROBERT JACKSON

'If I had yon horn in my kist,

Blaw, blaw, blaw winds, blaw

And the bonny laddie here that I luve best!

And the wind has blawin my plaid awa

Ye maun make me a fine Holland sark,

Blaw, blaw, blaw winds, blaw

Without ony stitching or needle wark.

And the wind has blawin my plaid awa

And ye maun wash it in yonder well,

Blaw, blaw, blaw winds, blaw

Where the dew never wat, nor the rain ever fell.

And the wind has blawin my plaid awa'

Andrew keeps the time, tapping his foot to the tune.

ROBERT JACKSON

'Now sin ye've askd some things o me,

Blaw, blaw, blaw winds, blaw

It 's right I ask as mony o thee.

And the wind has blawin my plaid awa

My father he askd me an acre o land,

Blaw, blaw, blaw winds, blaw

Between the saut sea and the strand.

And the wind has blawin my plaid awa

And ye maun plow 't wi your blawing horn,

Blaw, blaw, blaw winds, blaw

And ye maun saw 't wi pepper corn.

And the wind has blawin my plaid awa

When ye've dune, and finishd your wark,

Blaw, blaw, blaw winds, blaw

Ye'll come to me, luve, and get your sark.

And the wind has blawin my plaid awa.'

                    ELIZABETH JACKSON
        (clapping)

There's good lark in your work.

Now come and perch on the threshed quilt I've net,

Sit down now here, aye too, Andrew, ye all sutten[1],

The reap of the work hovers in the air here, hear,

The sways that remain, like ripples in the loch,

Of a song sung in innocence, ah, that your

Da' were here to eist[2], or our eldest, Hugh,

To keep the time and till the curve of us a'five,

A whole palm-hand plants five,

---

[1] sit
[2] listen

Yet ye twa[1] have yer place, 'tis true.

ANDREW JACKSON

Our place is on thy rug?

ELIZABETH JACKSON
(emotional)

Aye, tis sound, me brammers[2]... for now, for here,

Our Hugh is off to wager our freedoms on the stake

Of liberty, but I'd not have you twinning with him

There, noble as his brawf[3] that be. Andrew, Andrew

My babe gave to church. Say some such in churchy,

Wee minister.

ANDREW JACKSON
(quoting his Primer from memory)

Loquere, Domine, quia audit servus tuus.

ELIZABETH JACKSON

Aye there's my Andrew in eldest speech, aye that.

You'll sway our ways with tha wagging.

Now tuck in, tuck in! Now goodnight, goodnight.

Dream of the country coming...

Dreams...

---

[1] two
[2] term of endearment
[3] bravery

AMERIKAN REVOLUTIONS – 1780

Thunders on the night. Thunders roll the darkening day. March of red boots, march of blue boots. Bent legs struck off in a roll. War walks all the land. Hugh Jackson the first-born's first to fall to earth, sun struck. Those blank cotton fields, they burn black their smoke rises crooked the fetid air. A black sun in a noon day.

Look, Tarleton's Green Raiders march in ontop a white flag, stamping the fabric red, slash the hands held out in two.

THE JACKSON FAMILY CHURCH – SUNDAY, NOON

Thirteen gashes on the third man on the fifth pew. Seven on the second. The first, he's dead, no one pays his notice. Andrew, Robert, Elizabeth, they go into the church and dress some wounds with new knit rags and murmur prayers and peer for the fell'd Hugh. The wounded keep the church. A hymnal's held in rigor mortis. The congregation keep the wounded. They find the brother, Hugh, burnt dead on a pew. Brother, dear. Hold him. Andrew, roused, in a fury:

ANDREW JACKSON
(stomping his foot)
Now I will gird up myself and go down

To fight this Ablish' Giant that feeds on men!

ROBERT JACKSON

(wagging his leg)

I'll go with you, Andrew!

ELIZABETH JACKSON

(holding their legs in place)

Two more sons I'd lose today to the world!

Andrew, go to pulpit and preach, save the souls war

Send on ye, else be paralyzed on pews, as are these

Men that groan in outest darkness... Leave me not.

ANDREW JACKSON

(going up; hand on the pulpit)

These heard sermons were sweet. But now in this

Third space I hear tongues confounded to each

Particular wound as though the body

Of a man were itself an instrument,

Played by metals of cannon, ball, and blade

That turn a medley of groans from a gash,

And each scar a scale sounding atop Man.

Let tongues of fire now fall...

O call and answer, O psalm and communal

Lament. Here I leave my harp of weeping.

Pulpit, here, I take from you your voice. I talk

In carnages next. Altar, I pass over ye,

Bear arms for broken body, and drink blood

A'bitter till its drain.

ELIZABETH JACKSON

(*rushing at him*)

Nay, Andrew! I'll not let you! I'll-

ANDREW JACKSON

(*firing on her*)

-I heard my mission here!

*She's afraid, laves the church with tears. He comforts her
with her knit cloth as he leaves her. Robert went with him.*

A WAXHAW HOMESTEAD – NIGHT

*His cousin's killed. A lead ball was shot through the window
to lead through the tear of the cheek. Andrew looks on all his
red flow, minding on the floor, and fires blankly back, but the
night is dark. The redcoats, they are on the boundaries –
Andrew wrestles Robert to the floor – and they volley!*

ANDREW JACKSON

(*the balls crashing overhead*)

Keep that head without window. I've an aim.

*Andrew takes up the cavalry bugle from his cousin's puddle;
he steals out into the night.*

A MINUTEMAN

The yellow linkboy flees breakneck, pacing

To stone his luck in the slud-

ROBERT JACKSON
(shoving; shouting out the window)

-He steals to save us!

Fire the volleys! Wait on the cavalry!

Raise us up on wings like eagles, aye aye!

Crash on us, ye sea of red, coat us, brothers!

Fi fee fum fame! smell blood of Amerikan brain!

Andrew! Andrew! Don't leave me alone!

A MINUTEMAN (2)

Hold the boy down! Oh, woe! When a half-heights

Of us make the words of madness there's the

End of war, battle's true blank is babble…

A MINUTEMAN

Yes'sa! Wailing's a lifespan's wastrel! Thou, folly,

Why do we tarry in ye?

Minutemen might evacuate as soon's as

We congregate…

A MINUTEMAN (2)

Yup… On my word, tuck tail, fast a'foot.

Light. A bugle blares the Cavalry Charge through the night.
Clanging cast-irons. Redcoats, they flee like water away.

ROBERT JACKSON

The sword of the Lord, the arm of Andrew!

Enter, Andrew out the woods, holding his bugle, grinning
from ear to ear. Laughing in the air.

ANDREW'S AUNT'S HOUSE – MORNING

At that time, Andrew and Robert were sequestered with their aunt, a widow. A benign ambiance there, then Redcoats walk in. They level Andrew, wrestle Robert to the ground. They smash up the house, break up the belongings, the keepsakes, the pinebox and the old Scottish bureau. The aunt, a widow, she's wailing, a sound of war.

A REDCOAT OFFICER
(to Andrew; leering)

You, chinch[1], clean these mud'ed boots.

ANDREW JACKSON

You, crimp[2], you

Can lick 'em clean yourself.

Enraged, red, he raises his saber, splits the raised left-hand of Andrew, scrapes against his skull – a splitting headache. Andrew, his blood flees like water out. Robert charges up but is beaten down. But then, a marvel, Andrew stands slowly to his feet.

ANDREW JACKSON

Do that again.

---

[1] bedbug
[2] keeper of a low house, where sailors and emigrants are impressed to servitude on war ships

A REDCOAT OFFICER (2)

Stay! Hold that killing blow. This boy knows
His lay of the land, let this bloodhound dog
His friends hiding in the hills, on his life.

*His foes, they order Andrew to take the way up into the hills,
where the Amerikan Minutemen are. Robert went with him.
Andrew takes the long road around. He leads them by the
nose, to the road that is seen by the high-pitched tents. Just
so, the Minutemen get away, even in day.*

And Andrew, bleeding, laughs.

CAMDEN PRISON – RED EVENING

*No water in the low place. His blood is a dry scab on the
hand, on the head. The brothers, they lie, elbow to knee,
among the rows of the dying, furrows of the dead. Pox
engenders in pores, in the cells. Amerikan hollows. Andrew
files a hole in a board with a razor; they take turns breathing
through the hollow.*

*Elizabeth Jackson goes to the gate of the prison, a forty-mile
trail she blazed; she bargains with the Redcoats, begs.
Trades, three British men, for her two boys. They, the family,
head homeward. Andrew limps ahead, Robert slump over the
horse,*

24

half-dead. Elizabeth, she walks beside them, walking on grey weathered legs. No water.

Forty miles. And the weather wicked. Water in waves on their heads. Water in the pores in the cells the pox breeds humid the human shows on Robert the numerous little hills. Smallpox. In the tents, of Elizabeth and Andrew. They reach home and Robert is dead in his bed Andrew he lays dying there on the edge Elizabeth mopping his head with a soaked, knit, colored cloth.

ANDREW JACKSON
(whisper; somewhere between)

Raiments in the rain falling down, falling

Some fathom down, to mindings on the floor,

Enter into that, why don't you? Gather

That the slud of the flowing brains in hand,

Of cousins' course,

Window in his well he's well'd in windy rows,

Brother.

Mother.

Enter into that, you gab starstriker

(who offended you? that hence you're hearing?)

Leave me to pulpit pulse dead men on pews.

Leave me to live.

I gave me more turn to gasp through a prison chink.

Survivor.

The braille all on his skin, puss blinds his eye,

My palm brushing along his bumps, reading,

The uncountable hills, obituary.

Struggle to swallow these occupiers. Giant I.

Fo fum. Amerikan blood: Lug me Life.

Up.

THE FAMILY CABIN – MORNING

Andrew sits up in his bed. His skin, he checks, is smooth and clear. On his forehead, he checks, is a long red scar. Water is in his one hand, in the other, his mother's palm. He is well, full of Life.

She rises to leave him awhile. She says her last words.

ELIZABETH JACKSON[1]

Andrew, if I should not see you again,

Treasure up this word I say in your heart,

Take World for all in all, then make it your own,

Walk your own way, no man paths beside you,

Be friendly to all, forthright with not one,

Suspect the worst in men, yet seek their saint,

For their benevolence is roused in kind,

---

[1] this admonition based in part on Jackson's actual account, its dramatic nature leaves its verity suspect

Remember obligations as holy writ,

And politeness to an enemy, even

In war, raises up thy name in heaven,

Avoid quarrel, but in quarrels reveal

Aspects' lions that shake merciless manes.

Above all, to your own self be all in all.

She kisses his head, leaves for Charleston (some nephews imprisoned there), promises to be back in six days.

On the seventh, Andrew sat alone in the shade of the doorway, in the heat of the day.

Listen, SAHM rode up to him on a pony on her the clothes of Elizabeth are gathered in a bundle. He dismounts, lets down her clothes to him, sits beside him in the doorframe. A wailing there.

ANDREW

I'd like you to be with me now, always,

Not to leave me, ever, but be beside.

SAHM

Andrew, bring yourself out of your birthplace.

Leave your low places, to a land I'll show,

From your father's land, a fathering land,

From your name, a nation I mean to make,

From your person, a people without boundaries,

No time will be behind them, but before

Them, my embrace, a wide open abundance,

I through you, will bring this to a head.

I will make a greatness of you: Life, Name, Nation.

Bliss from you, blessing from blessers of you.

Death, famine, curses from cursers of you.

I mark your head.

I set my name on you.

Andrew brings himself out of the doorframe.

NORTH CAROLINA – THE TAVERN
MUDDLE'D MARK – NIGHT

A full house. Fizz through the slip of a cork. Andrew Jackson, a lawyer, crossed in, followed by three lawyerly mates. 'Thrice a swallie, keepy!'. Three low bars wall six long tables of function. Commerce, pocket men lean over, standing on the benches, shouting their hiked up prix'es for men, beaver, badger, bounder, a bale of cotton pyramid'ed on the table – a weasel's within. Politicks, a portrait of Saint George Washington stood on table nine pins arranged before the Majesty nine men (half Feddy's half Demos one Tory) roll the bowls along the table, 'cluclakt!' News, speaks!

ACT I   AN ANDREW JACKSON

*Three woodsmen hock gobbets and chors[1] into the jordan[2] on
the tabletop et swap their rip-tale roars[3]!*

NIMROD WILDFIRE

Iz good for a man to be shifty in a new country!

GRIZZLE NEWCOME
(loosing the gandershank)

If she new as'er sheen, e'no need da' drape'a
lambskin!

FIKE MINK
(standing on table)

E'ery woody knows tis sin t'trow way 'is
ammoonishin.

Fike Mink ne'er loses powder nor ball by my
vartuous

Eddikation I knews it so. I war out in de woods one

Arternoon down grate gap when I seed a rakkoon
setn

Lone onda tree so's clapped my Brown Betty up,
up, up

To the reddy to put my leady in when he lifted his
paw,

And sez, 'Is you Fike Mink?' I sez, 'You are rite for

Wonst, you blacc coon.' Sez he, 'You needn't take
no

---

[1] plugs of chewing tobacco
[2] a chamber pot
[3] tall tales

29

Farther tubble, Massa, fr I may well cum down n out, no

Nother werd.' Thar critter wilted rite down dat tree, for

He consiturd imself shot all-ready. So I's stoop down

And pats him on da head sez I I be shot myself before

I hurt a hare on y'a head, for I never had sich a kompli-

Mint in my life. Seeing as how u say dat says d'coon,

I'll jist jag off [1]fur t'present, lest Massa mind change.

NIMROD WILDFIRE

That varmint scamper?

FIKE MINK

Eyes winked an poof! Is hung up ded der in da tree!

Haw hee haw haw. A shaking of the bushwack[2]. Fire from.

Mouths. Terebinth the teacher the oak of Moreh grows from

their table strange fruit hanging there speaking

of sun.

---

[1] to slip away
[2] an ambush

ACT 1   AN ANDREW JACKSON

CHARLIE GOODNIGHT
*(pressing on a Jackworld in the
corner)*

Jack, O' why can't I wake you, Jack? Wake from thy

Wake, Jack. We need a Word in this wide World,

Jack O' Lantern Light. Turn the time.

A cockfight on the fifth table. In this corner, weighting five-pound, the seared Sechem. In this corner, weighting a whopping six-point-six point-six-pound, the tall black cockerel, Canaanite! A peck out of the eye, scumding[1] the comb by the beak, hatch, strut, mound of blood, like a yokel.

A dog tonguing the blood of the rooster. A Negro fiddler stamping his fine foot. Hessians smoking tobacco and winking, winking. Skirts spin upstairs.

The sixth table. Andrew Jackson has thereon arraigned a racecourse of spirits. He a lawyer and them his lawyers hoarse run the laps. Lapping. There is a Stranger at the head of their table. They do not notice em. Eir finger, rolling, slows the racy turning of the crazed tavern slow it down to a timely standstill.

---

[1] to scour, remove

IOSTAF

(silence; aside)

I brake the wheel to press an apology,

This Andrew is my own, a man in slant,

Hear, his story's deviant from history,

As time and their types are twisted in cant,

And I speak in sonnet, for soon Andrew,

My thin man sketch, with his trust in No-one,

A hand from the deck of love will draw

Queen riding on hearts, he shot like a gun,

Pierced by bullet of love, will topple fall

His life lived to lose, drop his love in life, die

What in him knows for naught the All in all,

He'll *live* Amerikan, all ends defy!

So let the tavern Wheel again revolve,

Time will re-turn, rise, trip, and so resolve.

The night darkens, a deeper night. A red lantern enters through the door, red light. Three scarlet women, in carnations, Andrew, hungry, he forks it over, in the tavern they wheel and dance and revolve. Scotch eggs. Brandy rum bum. Scandalon. Stumbles a rush of the uptight out the nightdoor to wide world. A blind veteran of the Revolution clutters over the block of a chamber pot, splits his spleen. Guffaws around. Andrew stokes the fire red like rubies,

melting, in the place of fire. Andrew in a rush rises and raises
an empty chair, hurls it into the fireplace.

ANDREW

I find you guilty of abandoning

Your betters, seat of seats, bearer of bums,

Faulty's, be sentenced to sit in hell!

His look-alike's also immolate their seats.

ANDREW
(running around)

Is there any else guilty in the court?

Aha! Drapes, you're accused of Mystery,

And since our punishments must hang on the crime,

Divorce from rack and window! Down, dark skirts!

Rip, tear, gather!

Since you veil us from light, nonce into light!

Tears down the draperies, tosses to the fireplace. Look-alikes
imitate. And Andrew kisses three in carnations on 3 red lips.

He takes up all the glasses on the tables, bundling them, in
his long, bone-thin arms.

ANDREW

Now these crystal carriers of spirit,

The hands to the clocking away of time,

The cups of the burden of the garden,

Watchmen to saps of eternity,

Liquors, which rise like flames our lower minds,

Thee I do love, and so I sentence ye,

Be loved 'ternally, marry fire's consummation.

*Glasses, third in fire's place. Burning sand a dark smoke up
the chimney aboving into the blank atmosphere. John Stokes[1]
stamps into the room, he bangs his silver doorknob gavel
hand against the grain and levels it on Andrew.*

JOHN STOKES

For the practices of the go-between,

For the immolation of the innocent,

For the banishment of the refugee,

For all thy warfare's songs of torment,

To walk in Fires of History I sentence ye,

In Devil's chronicle to be,

Till One who tolls to thee.

Andrew covers his face with his fists, turns to the fire.

ANDREW
(stumbling)

Where is the fourth in the furnace?

Where is the one who burns bright,

What is not burnt, in the fire's light?

---

[1] Andrew's mentor in the practice of the Law; his
hand was lost in battle against Indian tribes

I hear me, who *is* if not me?

Into the place of Fire, I'll go to burn,

All that is behind me, absence is.

Andrew, he walks into the fireplace – but is held back by his friends, wrestled to the ground, held there he moans and roars and the three in carnations dance in red, turning a tavern.

OUTSIDE – BEYOND THE MIDNIGHT

Andrew, bent double on himself, vomits on the ground. He wanders alone tilting down the road crossing onto a trail up a high hill, a clearing there. A rachel of rocks cairn'd, and stars fielded above.

There are some stones astray. Andrew pitched his knees, re-stacked those stones. Altar of the hill: East, West. Andrew, on his back, shows himself to the deep.

Hands, legs, widespread.

ANDREW

Sam... Sam... that is your name.

SAHM
(small voice)

I will give this canvas to you, even

Unto my stars of the morning, who sing

In the rising of the sun. Look on these,

A nation from you,

Numerous as spangled stars.

In the morning, Andrew journeyed down to Tennessee. There was famine in all that frontier. Andrew, he went further down to Nashville to live – starvation in that land, the West. Indians on the edge.

THE HOUSE OF RACHEL –
EVENING

In those days, it was not good for woman to be alone in the West. Now Rachel was lonely, lovely to look on. Robards, her husband, was fearful of other men, and jealousy green. He cast her out of his house. But look, he comes back to her, begs forgiveness, lodges with her at her mother's house. Andrew is there too, a lodger.

Andrew had looked longly on Rachel, how lovely. How she had rode the horse into the corral, how fetching. Her dark hair, her dark eyes, smile that dimpled in the pale cheek, falling into that.

You are as a sister to me, says Andrew to Rachel. So it was. That night, dinner – a lightning storm. Thunder.

ROBARDS

*(chewing dry biscuit
white as leprosy)*

Strikes me beyond the ear the bolts it does.

The thunder flashes seem to leap in home.

Burrr I said in the outhouse, what is this chill?

As if an augury'd holed into my heart,

But I leaned my head into the awk thing,

And saw I the cause, the cause it was, aye,

Black clouds 'ad gathered 'bove the timber lines,

But no natural weather, for these airy

Ornaments were not risen from the sea,

But sprung by my bed, bed, 'ad slunk across floor

Of moistened bedroom to fume up the chimney

And accumulate in air its horning its piping

Display, a double-backed blackness

This thunderstorm.

*Rachel sat at his left hand, Andrew at his right – the mother,
a third one, stranded in the corner of the room. A lightning
crash, its flash, a pale green light – brief. The venison cools
on the plates. Its antlers leer on the mantle. Flicker. Air
electric.*

ROBARDS

(to Rachel)

Now am I struck. Am killed. You, kept alive.

RACHEL

I will not abide this smoke. It is an

Acrid drama that you subject me to,

Your performance's dull with many showings,

I will not attend it. Enough, Robards.

Enough, sir.

ANDREW

I assure you sir my means and manner

Was, is, and will be always just. What you

Found us at was the punching of the saddle-

ROBARDS

-In the bedroom!? Fumid fulsome flamming-

ANDREW

-The rain, of which you've made much, drove us in.

ROBARDS

Droven in, droven in.

HER MOTHER

There's no inquiry.

ROBARDS

No question… Why have you done this to me?

RACHEL

Robards! I have done *nothing*! We have done

Nothing!

ANDREW

Done nothing in nothing, this' of nothing.

ROBARDS

(skin white like leprosy)

He's sone his deed in the hell of nothing!

RACHEL

Crass man! I'll say nothing under such suspicions.

ANDREW

(standing; to Robards)

And I'll not tolerate it. Let us speak on the porch.

A wall of rain out there on the edge. They stand, in flashes,

silhouettes of two men, one taller, thin, talling o'er the other.

ANDREW JACKSON

My character needs no defense to you.

You however, who by jealousies has

Once before banished a most innocent fair

Woman alone on the Frontier, where any

An Indian or silver-tongued knave could

Make his advantage, now raves out such an

Accusal as to heap back on your own head

The red coals of shame, what a husband's this.

ROBARDS

You're tha silver tongued th'makes his 'vantage on her,

You, lust, liar! A cheap lawyer. Chaser of the local

Petticoats, preyer on vulnerable women, married

Woman, would that ring of fire on her finger keep her

39

Caught within, but it burns the ringer by every thousand

Suitor leaping on, O pity, pity. You've already breached

Her keep I fear, yes, I fear. Narrow pit. Stranger woman.

ANDREW JACKSON

(quiet rage)

You will duel me, for honor, and her hand.

ROBARDS

Ah! Ah! More than her hand you mean, man, Oh this

Storm is me, heaps shames down on my house in stove

Buckets, no I'd not duel you, unchaste shot, no, I'd not,

I'd not – I'll dunk away into the drink, cast this lot me

Into the sea of whales! Look on the wife yours, Rachel,

Rahab, she's swallowed me, and she'll swallow thee!

He walks out into rain. Andrew, he walks into home.

This was good for Andrew. Rachel was a rich woman, dear and deep heart. They go together in the morning, to Spanish Natchez, elope there. On the rich banks, of Father of Waters, they stake their tent – he goes into her – her goes into he – a man and wife, one tent. Andrew, a household. Rachel, a wide field. Listen, her voice, it lays on the bank, mingles rises and falls on the murmurs of the waters of the flowing of the Great River, the Mississippi River, that Amerikan animated river.

RACHEL JACKSON

From the waters wide and deep a family

Will over'rush to the land a fertile earth,

My tall lean man, my arms explore your forms,

From the scar on your cheek, to the lines beneath,

Ah! Pommel, girth and cantle, nay and yay, lower,

Surround me, rush river running o'er

The banks of my rich hills, rush, rush, water.

And sow, and sower.

ANDREW

Dear heart… dear heart… Beyond the brim…

They rose out of Natchez, to Nashville, walking slow with their wealth. Andrew builds his practice there. He buys his first three people there, land of bondage, which they toil, a black soil.

MUSIC OF NASHVILLE – VARIOUS [1]

Tom twenty seven 60 pounds Aaron six years 100 pounds Peg maybe twenty six bought for services like clear those trees atop Hunter's Hill Cumberland Canebreak's twenty feet tall up der' and Injuns slip through it like they's water Thomas Fletcher and his two men all their skulls show red scalped all off on Duck river two more float like bloated rafts don't go out fetching for water, children. Widows, wait inside. Wait.

Roele 150 dollars Hannah with child Bet 80 pounds Betty with childs Hannah and Tom 125 pounds Mary 233 dollars two boys Swaney and Charles unspecified sum Suck 290 dollars slaves the slaves of Andrew Jackson, they go to and fro, driven, this way and that, along all Tennessee. Capital. Forming the earth. Mounding. George's sold down South, a lower land. He passes on his left hand the rachel of SAHM on the hill. He sees a large woman black sleeping there – in shade of the heat of the day – taller than ten feet tall she. He yearns, sings, to see her again. He goes down Southward.

Now look, Freddy was a slave of Andrew. Freddy, a middle-aged man, was a descendant of Ferdinando and Marigold.

---

[1] in this canto, slave names/prices are taken from their historical bills of sale

One day, he was walking through the tobacco fields by Andrew's side (for he was his overseer), and they were discussing the yield of crop and the yield of the hands.

FREDDY

Now you don't gotta be cautioning bout'

Showin' them th'firm hand holdin' the bitin'

Whip now, ol' Massa, you's a young Massa'

With a young heart biggin' and soften' to

Them and I's love you for dat, I do, sa',

But some of these niggas is liable

To advance advantages on ya', sa'.

ANDREW JACKSON
(*his mind occupied*)

Yes I thought so myself, Freddy, thank you,

You'll see to it that they feel my hand's firm?

FREDDY

Oh yes sa', yes sa', I'll spread the rumor

Like mule blood on bread, dog my cats ifn'I didn't.

ANDREW

I have never owned slaves before, Freddy.

FREDDY

Yes, sa'. Don't worry, I'll learn them to you.

You just show em your strength, they'll do the rest.

That's what Ol Freddy's learned, why when I was-

ANDREW JACKSON
(walking away)

-Bye, Freddy, bye now. Be seeing you, Fred.

FREDDY
(grinning; scowling; musing)

-Aye Massa, sunny days today now, sa'!

Massa young calf won't stand a straightening...

Issa' right smart piece from White to Massa

I say, sho don't seem t'know the way a'tall.

'Massa's in da blood, Massa', dat I'd say

And school and educatin' him ifn' he

Didn't like me playing and dancing the nigger

So much for him like we's some novelty

To the poor white trash crackerjack White boy

Dat don't know how his niggers form in kin

To be-kind to one another, and sho

Scrape their time off the top of da work like

A cuttin-razor shave. Well I'll whip em to it.

Massa's in da blood, and I've had some of

Dat in me from before I was born on all

Hallows, despite my dark, that's account' the

Massa's I've served right by their sides like dem,

Be myself a master of niggers, like I's

Could plant a plantation in Freddy,

So under a black sun da' cotton grow,

Then my Black would being White in wealth,
And them Blacks I'd eaten up for my health,
'Massa Ferdinando' I'll to the niggas show.
Yes I believe that's so… and say, dog my cats ifn'
It isn't, yes sa'! 'Yes Massa' I say to *myself*
Myself my massa. Hmf.

*Freddy speaks, and the slaves of Andrew obey, and the place
appears a plantation at last. Profits. Andrew speaks;
Tennessee becomes a State; Jackson, he is elected its first
Senator.*

PHILADELPHIA, USA – 1796

*The city's full. There is no more room. They've come to see
the President. The crowd, they crowd, Independence Hall.
Liberty, Liberty! Ring the bell. Here yourself through all the
land to all the Peoples thereof! Hear! The wound as from a
lance in its side sounds out its hollow ring but still the people
cast in the bell. They've come to see the President. Andrew,
standing there.*

*He lifted up his eyes: From the clocktower a newspaper
scroll unwinding, a head at its head down along the ground
to foot of crowd. A cloudy head. Voice from above like out a
wide well:*

VOX POPULI[1]

I a Citizen to administer the

Executives of Amerika am.

Though all my countrymen clothe me in their

Uniform trust where scarlet sacrifices

Stain my blues and white with patriot's mark,

I must decline thy animation…

For to the shades of age I so recline to rest…

A profundity presses now on me,

Yet this I'd press onto you, a Union

Twinly affection on thee perpetual be,

And our sacred Constitution's constant

Hand never depart its grip off thy heart,

But let spread freedom's blood to all nations

The permanence of thy felicity to Her.

More freedom, more power, with Liberty

Inwoven in e'ery limb and ligament

Until one body are, I now Name

You, Amerika, I estimate you,

Inestimable, inimitable imitator

Thy perseverance swerve!

Thou shalt frown down on any of the

---

[1] President George Washington gave his departing
address in the form of a newspaper article, distributed
throughout the country

Members that yearn to dismember of thee;

Thou shalt bolster the dollar's transaction;

Thou shalt not use any another tongue;

Thou shalt honor all thy founding fathers;

Thou shalt have one belief, manner, habit,

Politic and common cause.

The trumpets into one sound triumphing.

The North, in an unrestrained intercourse,

With the South, in the same intercourse,

With the North, and the East, in intercourse,

With the endless West, all in states combine.

Our word is present, living document,

May itself amend, as a flame its ends,

But with potent Fire, prudence itself be.

And there are engines from abroad. Cunning,

Ambitious, unprincipled men, East of

The Atlantic flood, who seek to usurp

Thy reins, and to raze, their own raisers up.

Europe, a very remote relation.

The Orient, a slumbering daemon.

Beware these kinds of men, that lie in kind,

Or in the skins of thee, as wolves do like

Lambs dress, will thee for its meal dress.

Beware these kinds of men: that of Party

Fashion their power, and agitates the

Jealousies of people in extremities,

Or use moralities as means.

Beware of such men as these.

Children, this' an offering to you, counsels

Of an old and affectionate friend.

Principles' shaped my ends, now guide you,

So there will never be a grave for you,

That you'd go down that plot of empires, but be

A Nation without end.

A Nation without an end.

Weary, I retire to the mansions of sleep,

To the clay of me, the fathers before,

And the father's after,

And all the rest,

The sleeping are

No thing.

The scroll rolls up the cloud fades the tower of the Hall shuts.
Andrew Jackson walks into the place where the President
was.

IN INDEPENDENCE HALL –
EVENING

George, an old man tall grey what was once his muscles hang
in flabs. He has no hair. His wig is on his knee. He has no
teeth. His dentures rest in the scalp of his dry wig. He sits in

the shadow of the Liberty Bell. He's covered in blankets – his slaves cover him. They motion Andrew to come up to him, leave them alone.

GEORGE WASHINGTON

Cloudy my head is in the last of days,

In patches, my sun shines through, to sweep lands

Below, lending my heat to bud the Spring.

Andrew, I would bless you.

Andrew, he kneels before him an old grey hand in a young wild shock of standing red hair.

GEORGE WASHINGTON

First in war, first in peace, first in the hearts

Of our Countrymen I am, shall the lands

Transgress against itself? And shall the slave

Ensnare his master? Where is Andrew?

ANDREW JACKSON

                                           Under

Your hand.

GEORGE WASHINGTON

Andrew, his eyes shall be red with a wine,

Andrew, his teeth shall be white with a milk.

But on barren bough I see a shape is set,

Which will not fall nor unlet, there it hangs,

On ropes of sand the body, chasing wind,

It is the toll, a bell

Above is crashing its hand 'gainst its side:

'Where are the sons of Liberty?

'Where are the sons of Liberty?

Find me! Andrew!'

I do ebb now…

The things I foresee, over the edge of

The prow, would stun us all to silence…

So it was. As quickly as he went to Washington, Andrew left it, back homeward to The Hermitage.

THE HERMITAGE – 1806

Freddy'd addressed himself master of the place in place of his Master, Andrew's absence. Freddy is strutting among the fields, the cock of the walk, looking this way and that at Baruni a young black girl reposing under a hickory tree in shade of the heat of day.

FREDDY
(*sauntering up*)

Now miss Baruni why's you set settin

Under the shadin tree now, you know's is

A sin to squander your energies o'day.

BARUNI

(sarcasm)

Massa Ferdinando-

FREDDY

-Don't curl that lip.

BARUNI

I'd grin and it'd mean just the same mean thing.

FREDDY

What's that?

BARUNI

Massa Ferdinando ain't no

Massa at all, Massa Ferdinando's

But a mean old niggerin nigger man,

Dat Andrew could hold out a collar and

You'd pout and lap like a hound-dog for it.

Freddy leaps on her, turning her over, hitting her on the back, whipping his hand, barking, barking.

BARUNI

Ah! Ah! Stop! Please! No no no no no! Ah! Stop!

FREDDY

(heavy breathing)

Little darky… lil darky… Educate you…

Enter, Rachel Jackson, rushing from the shaded porch.

RACHEL JACKSON

Freddy! Freddy! You stop that right now, Fred!

She goes up, tries to pull him off. He places a palm on her.
No more than a slight push. He comes to his senses sees what
he's done shouts out in fear and regret & bows to her.

FREDDY

Mistre-mistress, Freddy didn't know what he done,

He didn't mean to it, he didn't mean to it, missus.

I'm sorry, I'm awful sorry.

RACHEL

You touched me,

I oughtta have you whipped worse than you've

Done to Chil' Baruni there.

FREDDY

Yes missus,

Whip ol' Freddy good for what he done.

RACHEL

Quit. Grovelin, even in a slave,

Is no fine sight. Now we've agreed that while

Master Andrew is gone I've charge of the

House slaves, while's you've charge of field hands,

Is that so, Ferdinando? Answer me, boy.

FREDDY

Yes mam, that's how it is, for your sake you

Don't need be dealing with these lazy niggs

Out in the heat all days like I do missus-

RACHEL
(raising her hand)

-Baruni's now my house negro, she'll be

My personal servant, you understand?

FREDDY

…Yes mam.

BARUNI

Look horizon'ly, Miss.

Andrew Jackson was returning from Washington. They see him approaching.

FREDDY

Mistress, is you gonna tell him

Now bout what I'd done here today, missus?

She doesn't answer him, runs out to Andrew to meet him there.

BARUNI

She's gonna tell him, Freddy.

FREDDY

What's that, girl?

BARUNI

She's gonna tell him you laid your hands on

His wife and he's gonna cut you off to a stub

Nigger-hood, then ya hands, ya tongue too, Freddy.

FREDDY

You hush now.

BARUNI

You hush now. You ain't massa

To me no more, Ol' Freddy, and I wouldn't wish

To be y'a, cuz if she don't tell him right now

It'll be another time, on any slip of anger

Or caprice nod she'll spill the beans on y'a,

And you'll be sold down the river without

A pecker-

He hits her hard across the lip.

FREDDY

-I'll kill you dead, girl. A peckerless negro's

Capable of all kinds of caprice.

Baruni runs off into the big white house.

THE PORCH OF ANDREW – SUNSET

His hands are tending his fields, the burgeons of crops. In the rocking chair, Andrew calls for Freddy. He runs up to him.

FREDDY

Yes, Massa.

ANDREW JACKSON

Thank you for managing the

Hands of my field, Freddy. I won't be at

Washington anymore.

FREDDY

Yes, Massa.

ANDREW JACKSON

Did you encounter any difficulty

In showing 'a firm hand to our hands', Fred?

FREDDY

Oh this a fine crop of niggas you's got

Here Massa. It weren't no trouble once I

Showed them you wouldn't be taking no lip nor

Lounge lazin under the hickories, sa'.

ANDREW JACKSON
(imitating his accent)

Then you have straightened out the crooked, sa'?

FREDDY

…Yes, Massa, even-straight as a river reach.

ANDREW JACKSON

Then, since that's so, I'll be selling you to

New Orleans in the morn, first thing.

FREDDY

Yes, Massa.

Thank you very much, Massa.

ANDREW JACKSON

Thank you? Why?

FREDDY

Well if you's dismissin me sa' then you

55

Have no need of me then Ol Freddy's done

His duty, which was to bring up his Massa

In the way he was to go, for this exile

A mighty powerful message sends to

The slaves that'd pull prerogatives with you,

Now families will fear a fracturin again

And be good for you and mistress Jackson.

A slave's happy in service, sa'.

ANDREW JACKSON

By the eternal… That's very wise of you to say.

FREDDY

Wisdom's not taught, but caught in the whips, sa'.

ANDREW

I won't have you sold to someone wicked…

FREDDY

Is you going to New Orleans with me?

ANDREW

No…

FREDDY

So someone that's not Massa's gwyne sell me…

ANDREW

Yes…

FREDDY

An' they may be someone wicked, an' Massa

Knows the wicked love only the wicked,

And would sell ol' Freddy to each other.

ANDREW JACKSON

I'll get his word to sell you to a good

Man, now that will be all, Freddy.

FREDDY

Oh yes Massa that'll be all and thank you

Again for all your kindness and goodness,

You's the best Massa Ol' Freddy's eve'had,

He's had so many. Now you want me to

Go grab and get the three hens now?

ANDREW

Three hens??

FREDDY

(grinning)

Well yes sa', the three hens for the bribin', sa'.

ANDREW

The bribe?

FREDDY

Yes sa' you said you's gwyne get

The flesh trader's word on the exchanging,

Well, he won't be liable to take that good on free.

I think th' three hens under the arm oughta strong it.

ANDREW

... And if I wasn't agreeable

To bribery with three hens, what then, Fred?

FREDDY
(*clucks his tongue*)

Oh yea that is a steep price Massa, well

What I could do is just… sell myself, sa'.

ANDREW

You would sell yourself, Fred?

FREDDY

            I would fetch a

Good price for myself, get you a good deal

Despite all the mileage on me, and the

Scars and the bruises and the whippin tongue,

And I can spot good Massas from bad like

I can find a trail of pig tracks, so you

Wouldn't have to go worrying all your nights

About me being sold down the ol' riva' to a

Wicked man, no sa', I could take that weight

Off your shoulders, I could… an' onto mine.

*They look at each other for a long while, eye to eye. Andrew
rises out the rocking chair. They stand face to face.*

ANDREW JACKSON
(*a low voice*)

We are wily both, and so brothers by

That bond. Come, let's not quarrel. You may let

Yourself go, face the whole country, and meet

Your own way in it, I'll not interfere,

Andrew Jackson lets Ferdinando go,

But remember that by *me* it was so.

So Freddy turned and looked on all of Amerika; lifted up his eyes, looked on the low plains of the South the wetlands swamps rivers and all the gardened life there fertile even unto the cities of the plain: Richmond, Atlanta, Charlotte, New Orleans.

He staked his eyes on New Orleans. East of Andrew.

Andrew, he lifted up his eyes, Rachel there. He goes up into her. Thenon, he is made the head of the militia of Tennessee.

THE HERMITAGE, TENNESSEE – 1806

Andrew Jackson meets Aaron Burr[1]:

AARON BURR

Even now the Spanish, French, English,

On these boundaries encroach to grow Empires

On the fat of the land unconquered,

---

[1] Burr had fled to Tennessee after his deadly duel with Alexander Hamilton. Meeting Andrew Jackson, the two would discuss Lewis and Clark, Western expansion, conspiracy, and the imperial powers

So may I present the instruments of the

President, who would marry East with West.

Enter, spirits of Meriwether Lewis and William Clark.

ANDREW JACKSON

Tell me what you've seen.

LEWIS

Where each mountain has its secret meaning

We went. Our expedition began in

Pennsylvania, there a forty foot

Pirogue is purchased for the odyssey,

And rigged and righted for a journey

Full of awe, full of woe.

CLARK

Falls of the Ohio, 'Good River', we go the

Ways down to join our Ciconian York,

He bore her off, flames of love force on force,

No more complicated a man you'll meet

Than our black Ciconian York, than our

Crew of bold explorers sailing a veiléd breeze.

LEWIS

A winter spent under fortress of trees,

The hearth burns lotus buds that shall not cross

The Continental Division, of time

And space, to creating Vision, the bois

Tears the veil of the river by the prow,
The personall in the impersonall stream.

CLARK

Kaw Points on Kansas we set stakes in caves,
Doors to forebode the Savages yet the
Inhospitable Eye does not wink when it
Administers a hundred, hundred
Lashes or more on its own wooly back.

LEWIS

On the Big Bend we'll arrange to meet my
Great White Father, bagg'd winds sailed us to the
Lakes of the Dakota. A tumescent
Canoe on a fecund body of water-

CLARK

She rose from she, Sakakawea, she
Like the looming moon wove a way for
Pompy the conqueror bourne through her legs,
Motherhood is itself an end, Kirke,
We will water you red now O' sea of grass,
Where the buffalo moan and the grizzly
Bear like a tower is toppled low. And the
Furs be skinned and the scalps be trapped and the
The rail, of the coming industry, will
Track their times like braces on the land that
Was yours, but is now ours the land,

So it was,

But still she, Sakakawea, save her—

LEWIS

She, eld as the leaves that autumn,

Calmly recovers the Word that fell

Into her wide river, Kirke, of herbs

And of honor, is taller than snowy steeps

Of the Rockies, younger than their new

Mountain snows, first beheld in white eyes,

By her grace beheld, her babe held remembers

The Giant Woman how her Great Falls divide,

Niagara,

The World outer into Under. Recognize,

On the Point of Rocks, the dead being as

The rocks being as the dead, the Being

Of the dead: reunion of inunion.

CLARK

To Cameahwait[1] a great black ram we give,

He'll burden the elusion of the Earthshaker,

Who props up, in vapors, his illusion:

Ocean ends us, the first of delusion.

LEWIS

So our journey ended.

---

[1] brother of Sacagawea and a Shoshone chief

CLARK

The return our

Journey mended, great gifts to President

We to him presented.

AARON BURR

A President by deception elected...

ANDREW JACKSON

The woman who led you, what became of her?

LEWIS AND CLARK

We've adopted her son!

AARON BURR

The People are the crown of an Amerikan King...

ANDREW JACKSON

That return, from coast to coast, will belt us

A fatherland, a sonland, round as a waist,

What a wide wide-open country she is.

LEWIS AND CLARK

She – is – in – always – are!

THE HERMITAGE – LATER THAT
NIGHT

Remember the Word. They are alone together.

RACHEL

I've no son to round this waste,

To grow a globe of me to world us,

What is the point of Promise when each grain

Of expectation planted comes to dust

Of months? Death without children, the legacy

Left to drain out to servants and on slaves?

He turns her – face to face.

ANDREW

The barren is of me.

RACHEL

No, it's me.

The moon has passed its mid, and middle age

Wanes in me, I've given us naught all, naught all,

Nothing you've won me from him for-

ANDREW

-Hush, dear heart, hush-

RACHEL

-No, I will beat what's within.

Sam's held me back. I have an African

Maid, Baruni, go into her, our slave,

And a child for you will come out of her.

ANDREW

No...no... no...

He quiets her with his mouth, a fire burning there.

HARRISON'S MILL, KENTUCKY – DAWN[1]

Andrew receives the fire of the man who raises his shaky arm and shot which broke through the breastbone and the third rib of Andrew, yet Andrew does not sway. He raises a halfcocked trigger (fired twice) – and the man is on the grass.

Inreunion. His wife races there, but to bury and to wail. Andrew's laid up in the upper bedroom to bleed through three mattresses through three nights. Rachel there:

RACHEL JACKSON

Only what flows between your legs inhers',
She is a deep well, look to at night the stars,
So your kin will be as countless as these.

An Andrew Jackson lays on the edge of his deathbed.

---

[1] this song recounts the first of Andrew Jackson's many duels, legal at the time in Kentucky

ACT II

THE 1ST DREAM OF ANDREW JACKSON

A dispute over some horses a hoarse shout for honor in the leaves & the man lies on the grass lying that he'd stir the line of confusion or the stones of emptiness I pinch the bullet that remains a rock lodged in the slump of my shoulder head us down heartward.

Down the hill of the Hermitage. Slaves there on the bank of the brook dancing naked in and out its lap I stand above (in flared frock coat which hugs my broom frame and the medal of my rank flares with the fine shirt she sewed) hands on hips leer I answer

ANDREW

Little Red, I told you to wash the trough.

LITTLE RED
(*swaggers up th'bank his dangling*)

Massa Jackson, I done told y'a I was

To press da riva' stones unda my feet,

S'a, so dat da riva' wine nice and clear

Down the mound of her ven, s'a us.

67

ANDREW

Aye. Why these that tread the press naked?

LITTLE RED

We was always here, Massa man. Eye.

THE BLACK BATHERS

We's always here, laughing in da' riva',

Treading wine from smooth stones,

Tread the wine with us from these stones.

ANDREW

Little Red, prepare my horse, neigh.

He slumps all four limbs on the grass (clutching its green hair pulling deftly delicately). Andrew Jackson sits on his back clucks his tongue his heels in the derived ribs poke in.

ANDREW JACKSON

Go forward, git'.

LITTLE RED

I will buck you, rider.

The man and the rider into the brook plashing the bathers laugh at the absurd plash their water on Andrew on Red with songs by the breadth of their lungs.

ANDREW JACKSON

Do not get me wet, I do not like that.

THE BLACK BATHERS

There is an off spring hidden in all things.

Galloping down the brook widening into a river Andrew afraid curls into his hair the trees leer and lean and snag (his hat lost and his frill, medals rust as his clothes unloose). The river into a ravine the strong bluffs above red shaped with to face the ages of the wind and an ancient seabed.

James Madison and Others mount the bluffs.

HENRY CLAY

War with Albion will birth out a babe.

JOHN C CALHOUN

The South shall wax into a yellow moon,

Who is da man of da South, where he noddin?

HENRY CLAY

Who'll cut the Giant's head, he shall be king.

JAMES MADISON

Whom shall I send, who will go for us?

ANDREW JACKSON

Me!

Surge of the waters into a valley his hearse man bucks him off at bottom. Desert. Seven black horses cut in two along the spinal canal and is laid on the tabletop rock. Andrew buck naked watches the fresh cuts. He flaps and chases away the crows that land to eat, flapping his long thin white freckled and flushing arms till he tires, turns, down to a curled sleep.

Tecumseh[1] stomps his wide foot; the desert shakes like a

Woman in labor. From the red dust that is thrown up comes
The Noise Maker, Lalawethika[2], one eyed, arrows in his
earlobes, in his hand a bone knife in his nose a bone &
burning feathers thro' the rings hooked in his lips he spits
wyrd:

LALAWETHIKA

By my mighty medicine Muscogee,

Blood will turn from white to red, and the axe

Will again an edge and the arrows in

Your fathers' side will out for they cry out

That the White race is not eradicated.

Seventeen fires of the Amerikan

Colonies I see o'er leap their boundaries

And all those flames their tinder'ers consume

The White House is burning!

All Washington is a house for the owl,

And a roost for the dragon, the jackal,

There is not a speck of White on the land,

Not a suggestion of his Blank, for the

---

[1] Shawnee chief who prompted resistance to United
States expansion onto Native American lands
[2] Younger brother of Tecumseh, a religious leader of
the Shawnee tribe, known as 'the Shawnee Prophet'

Place of him knows him no more, wind passing,
And grass re-growing, and the Indians
Growing from the grass they were, are, will be,
Ever the grass.

Andrew clutches the dust looking for the horses that are cut.

LALAWETHIKA
(following)

Your seed are strangers in a land not theirs.
So I soothsay, slavery will be their state,
Listen, four hundred years it will be so,
A State of slavery, the nation which
Enslaves will know judgement, and will come out
Prosperous, proud, backs with their wealth bowed,
Wandering, roaming with heavy weight,
Into a desert without
Rain.

Darkness. A smoking furnace a bright burning coal in midst producing pushing Blackness – a burning lamp – leaps between the twins of the severed parts of the seven horses.

Great River. Andrew stands at prow his soldiers row him forward into the country he sees all contours to come, the rails wedding, the props measuring, the steam gin breathing – snag on a sawyer,

falling into water

Inwater.

SAHM

I gave you this land, even from the East

To the shores of Oregon, from the tribes,

Cherokee, Crow, Algonquin, Pequot, to

The Kingdoms of the Aztec and Maya,

To the European usurpers, the

British, Spanish, French, and the Dutch,

From the Masters to the Slaves,

All this, yours, for yours.

Go through the gates.

Land of the archers[1]. Benton brothers draw their pistols, fire, Andrew's struck in the shoulder an artery severed bullet in his left arm and he's laid up in a bed. He'll whip a man that'd amputate that arm. He bleeds until he dries out. The arm stony a cast he lies on a stack of thoroughly red mattresses.

---

[1] Andrew Jackson's second duel ended as the first

FORT MIM, ALABAMA – AUGUST 30, 1813

They leave their gates open. They watch their children play in the yard. Two black slaves wander into the forest. As is their custom to roam. Look, they see painted Indians moving like streams of color through the trees. The two black slaves, they run back to the fort, warn them, and are flogged by them. But when the dinner bell rings the whoop goes up to toll that the colored stream is rushing in – they left their gates open.

They were naked, painted black and red, wore cow tails hanging down between their legs. Red Sticks. War club, tomahawk, spike, arrow, torch, burning fire. They cut them down those that flee the smoke from the wall and the caved in roof. They cut them down the women, children, even as their protectors fled like blood through a hole carved in the board. All are stripped. Some are raped. All are scalped.

The women the girls their sex is laid severed on themselves beside the abortions which they made, which are caused on them to see. They take the Blacks for slaves of their own. They drain away, into the forest where they came, like streams of color black and red, now blacker, now redder.

A survivor who fled sends a message to Andrew Jackson, 'Five hundred dead they are hidden on our edge muster for war.' Life on the frontier, so it was.

THE BACKWOODS – 1813

Now Andrew Jackson had summoned some five thousand volunteers to join him, so Tennessee is called The Volunteer State to this very day. They marched through the woods. Hunting men. Andrew led the column mounted on his white horse, his second in command, John Coffee, was on his right hand.

ANDREW JACKSON
(muttering)

Boldly into the Indian I go,

For I've stitched our anger into our sail,

To sail as a ship of death to their shore,

Crouching there, grinning there, with the fire

Of Amerika summoned to their

Tented fields, staked on my very palm, here

They war with me, mar for me, men of me,

Burning brands in all our hands, cleanse us out

All the Indian on the edge.

These sharp wars will wake a name of Jackson.

Meanwhile, at the back of the column:

FIKE MINK

Eager for the dead doing deed, burn all, burn all

Pile corpse in little hills, here be heads, deoppilate

The population, of the continate. Hear ye!

NIMROD WILDFIRE

Why does the general ride us as a hushed head?

DAVY CROCKET

The affairs of war afflict a general tete[1]

More than the smashinest[2] general muster,

His spumy thoughts are our silent doing's.

NIMROD WILDFIRE

You swink[3] that so?

DAVY CROCKET

May I run on a sawyer if I didn't,

May pizzen burn in my lariat t'night

If Davy Crocket speak slantindicler[4],

That's teetotal truthin'!

NIMROD WILDFIRE

Say Davy, ain't you too young to hunt men?

DAVY CROCKET

If bravery's measured by the beard, then any

An old goat's got the edge on man, Nimrod.

---

[1] head
[2] superlative of exciting
[3] to reckon
[4] to speak obliquely; falsely

SAM HOUSTON
(babying Pope's Iliad in his arms)

Sing, muse, now of the man above all men!

Descend, Mnem. Recall an Andrew Jackson!

'There, far apart, and high above the rest,

The Thunderer sat; where oddly Olympus shrouds

His hundred heads in heaven, and props the clouds.'

Yet our Andrew Ares, war god, war man,

Should be cheery in the passion of war,

I say we sing, rouse up our martial songs

To stoke from his our general heart.

A SOLDIER (1)

Old Hickory, he's thin but tough to break!

A SOLDIER (2)

Sing a song for Old Hickory! Voices!

DAVY CROCKET

You can't keep a good man down! Sing it out!

SAM HOUSTON
(singing loud, others join in)

'Ye gentlemen and ladies fair,

Who grace this famous city,

Just listen, if ye' et time to spare,

While I rehearse a ditty;

And for the opportunity,

Conceive yourselves quite lucky,

For tis not often that you see,

A hunter from Kentucky!'

ALL SOLDIERS

'Oh! Kentucky, the hunters of Kentucky,

The hunters of Kentucky!'

John Coffee nudges Andrew to listen. General Jackson bends his ear to them, grins, bravo's them along. They whoop, shout, sing, stream their color through the trees.

DAVY CROCKET

'We are a hardy free-born race,

Each man to fear a stranger,

Whate'er the game, we join in chase,

Despising toil and danger;

And if a daring foe annoys,

Whate'er his strength and forces,

We'll show him that Kentucky boys

Are alligator horses!'

ALL SOLDIERS

'Oh! Kentucky, the hunters of Kentucky,

The hunters of Kentucky!'

They near the village, Tallushatchee, of the Creek. Go in, cavalry, reduce, reduce, sing as you do.

SAM HOUSTON

'I s'pose you've read it in the prints,

How Indians attempted

To make Old Hickory Jackson wince,

But soon his scheme repented;

For we with rifles cock'd,

Thought such occasion lucky,

And soon around the General flock'd,

The hunters of Kentucky!'

ALL SOLDIERS

'Oh! Kentucky, the hunters of Kentucky,

The hunters of Kentucky!'

They cross over the boundary. They encroach upon them as storms, setting torch to teepees driving the women and children into circles butchering the men burning the corn.

ALL SOLDIERS

'They found at last 'twas vain to fight

Where lead was all their booty,

And so they wisely took to flight,

And left us all the beauty!

And now, if danger e'er annoys,

Remember what our trade is,

Just send for us Kentucky boys,

And we'll protect you, Ladies!

Oh! Kentucky, the hunters of Kentucky!

DAVY CROCKETT

Level them! Sing ditty as you slay!

SAM HOUSTON

All is guts and glory! All is absurdity!

176 dead on the field and 80 prisoners sent to White schools for learning mending and more. While his men lounged on the ashes and dove their heads in water to drink from the creek,

Andrew wandered about the ruined village, his wild red head leaning down. Remember, Rachel Jackson bore no children. Then, Andrew had only grasped her. Now, Andrew conceived and grasped her words, and he came into the teepee – an infant wailing on ash there a Creek boy, Lyncoya – Andrew, he takes the babe up into his arms cradles him walks over his dead,

And sends him home to Rachel.

THE HERMITAGE COTTON FIELDS – MIDDAY

Baruni, her breasts swell'd to nurse the Indian adopted babe and she's put up in an upper room where she begins to look down on Rachel who's only rounded with fat and old age.

BARUNI

*(swaddling Lyncoya; gadding
through the cotton fields)*

Now it's der' dat God lives, in da ground der',

See how they sow Him wid der' hands, baby?

Now da' sower knows his seed as well as

Da' hand, both are black, of the earth, and a

Black man's palms is pale so's he can see of

Earth he hold der', dat he is der', da' black

Man knows da earth better than anyon else,

He is da' Fadder, da' sower, while the White

Man is just da' black birds dat come and steal

Some of da' seeds, and da' black man just smiles

And shakes his 'ed and says, White man, you'll be

In da' earth too, haha, Earl will be Earth,

And sumtimes da' hard sun that made da' black

Man so black with his love will come along

And dry up da' summa seeds, choke em out,

And da' black man just smiles and shakes his 'ed

And says, now listen here old hard sun, and

Listen good ol' sun, you's a summoned thing,

You may choke my seed but you'll be but a

Seed one day too, ya'hear? When our Chariot

Comes o'er dat holy mountain we won't

Need of y'a segregatin' light, and you'll

Go on and dive yerself into da sea,

An steam-up all dat it's cover'd up, dat sea,

And da black man will be der' sowin dat

Fresh green pasture der' dat was the seabed,

And da' White man'll be right beside him too,

Cuz da sower neva' goes, mm, mhm,

Listen to dat, da Sower neva' goes.

Baby, you's gonna grow up to goad dese'

Sowers here, so you hear me when I say,

You treat em' all like dey was da Savior,

For der' backs is bent closer to God dan

Da White man's is, dey's da Sower an da' Seed.

Rachel calls her in from the porch. Baruni, she keeps going making the long way around the fields. Rachel calls her in. Still, she keeps going. She comes around, and then comes in.

RACHEL

Sit down there, Baruni. Now stand up here.

Now walk in a circle. Now spin. Again.

When I say you do you do it, girl. Hear?

You remember well and good how you're saved

By me from the fields and don't think you can't

Be sent right back to shucking and picking.

You hear me now, slave girl?

BARUNI

Yes, yes, missus.

RACHEL

Now give him to me.

BARUNI
(loosing her abundant breast)

He's still hungry, missus.

THE TENTS OF ANDREW JACKSON,
THE BACKWOODS – DAY

On the campaign trail, AJ's men are starving to death. They are looking for Indians, the Red Sticks, who did-in Fort Mims. AJ, sick, always on the edge of sickness, full of parasites, shivers in his tent. John Coffee bursts in:

JOHN COFFEE

Mutiny! The volunteers'll be marching in the

Morning! they'll flee right over our feet,

Bring the brigades with em!

General Jackson! The army will be dissolved!

ANDREW JACKSON
(standing sickly to his feet)

Have the betraying brigade assembled

In formation with all, and prepare the

Artillery to fire, on me.

Andrew Jackson, hiding his sickness, walks along the line of his forces. The artillery is ready to fire point blank upon the mutinous brigade. Jackson stands in the cannons mouth.

ANDREW JACKSON

We stand on the verge of the great battle,

You must decide whether you'll flee the enemy,

Or flee from me. See the canon. Persist

In your determination to mutiny,

And you must pass over me and the mouth.

I'm not afraid to meet my end, nor make

Such an end as to swallow my own men,

Death before dishonor.

The point between us shall soon be decided.

     (he waits; no response)

Artillery, light the match, and ready to

Obliterate us patriots.

They surrendered to him and his ways.

He led them the way up to the field of battle, a Creek village. Sharp Knife[1]. John Coffee and Davy Crocket lead the force, surrounding the village, with fires in their mouths.

---

[1] the nickname given to Jackson by the Creek. It stuck that way forever

Indian women and children they come out to surrender they are gathered in a bundle. The Indian men they take refuge in a house and fire arrows. Jackson watches from his horse.

DAVY CROCKET

Don't fire! Do not fire! Hold that dander down!

Take care of the women and children first,

Round em into a heap, lasso em here,

Then move onto the men.

One of the women who is touched many times she's hid a bow down her buckskin jacket and an arrow along her arm, there she takes it out kills the man beside Davy. He cannot hold them back. They, the Natives, are butchered. They, the Amerikans, surround the holdout house, set flame and agony.

ANDREW JACKSON
(atop his pale horse)

Elegant fire, such elegant affair…

Davy Crocket and his men they come back under the night cover. Starving. They have heard that potatoes were stashed under the fired house they open up the boarded-up walls – Indian men, red with their burning, dissolving there.

They push them aside in bundles, dig up the ground. Potatoes there, soft, of an oil unction'd on them. Davy only eats a little.

Then it is very cold. The snow falls like ash through the empty
air, moving, revolting like a stomach without bread. Hunger.
Andrew (woe that the fight needs be fed) sends them home.
They go like streams hungry through the creeks and the trees.

THE HERMITAGE OF THE LAMB –
NIGHT

Rachel comes upon Andrew on the porch in the winter night.
A homely fire there. Andrew is before it, a lamb and a babe
between his knees. He starts at seeing her.

ANDREW

Lyncoya cried out in the night, the cry

Of the lamb in the cold at night, woken

Him up to it. He requested I warm

Them both up, he is me, I thought he meant.

Isn't that the heart of innocence, dear heart?

RACHEL

I ache on behalf of you, heart.

ANDREW

                    Why, dear?

RACHEL

Sam's judged between you and me, split us oe'r

My empty waist, so my wrongs are right on top

Of you, when you conceived my words and got

This red ward on the black slave then I was

Lower than both.

In Baruni's eyes I am below.

Andrew looks down on Lyncoya's face, sleeping by the lamb.

ANDREW JACKSON

The slave to you I gave. Your property.

Do with her what you will.

RACHEL JACKSON

Dear heart, I will.

Morning.

*Forty lashes under the hard sun. Lines leave on the back.
Baruni flees low under the high eyes of Rachel. A runaway
slave running from a frail tree.*

Into wilderness.

Andrew makes love to Rachel, but there's no affair there.

Andrew returns to warfare.

THE BACKWOODS CAMP – LATE DAY

ANDREW JACKSON
(running about his tent)

Which is the damned rascal! Shoot him! Shoot him!

Blow ten balls through the damned villain's body!

Bring me the body of the traitor, John!

JOHN COFFEE

The boy's been disarmed, he remains imprisoned.

Andrew takes out his pistol, bangs the butt of it on the table.

ANDREW JACKSON

I will court marital him, John, I must,

For the mettle of the men, make example.

Who was there, impartial, saw the offense?

JOHN COFFEE

That would be that young grit, Sam Houston, sir.

ANDREW JACKSON

Send him in to me at once.

JOHN COFFEE

Aye General.

Sam Houston into the tent, in a coonskin hat his powder horn around his neck his Iliad under his arm his moccasins from his Cherokee father on his feet. He stands before the General.

ANDREW JACKSON

Tell me what occurred with John Wood.

SAM HOUSTON

The boy was on picket duty this morn,

His commanding officer permiss'd him

To morning victuals, there he was eye'd

By 'nother officer, who inquired

To his slackin' off of duties, the boy

Answered as any Kentuckian would, sir,

With a rip-roaring curse, a curse for all

The ages of bronze man, a fight then broke,

With the breaking of nose and the boy 'fendin

His person with his Brown Bessy, he was

Disarmed amicly by his friends, who'd heard

Of your anger at the situation.

Might I ask, General, what you mean do

With the wild boy?

                          ANDREW JACKSON

                    He comes from the mutinous

Company, I've little say but to swing him

On the gallows' ropes, a crashing symbol.

                          SAM HOUSTON

Mercy sir can speak much more fine, please y'a.

                          ANDREW JACKSON
          (sitting)

You're young Sam, my boy might be your age,

As might this wild man, John. I weep for his

Passing, I do, but 'tis the inevitable

Course for his sin's consequence. That'll be all.

                          SAM HOUSTON

I've a piece of my mind to speak first, sir.

ANDREW JACKSON

Please do.

SAM HOUSTON

Well sir, d'situation seems to me
Commensurate with the 'ol saying I
Once heard of an ol' Knacker bull, timeworm
And mossgrown: 'Ye are to be hanged, boy, and
I hope it will prove a warning to ye'.

ANDREW JACKSON
(laughing)

What'd ya mean, Sam?

SAM HOUSTON

Well, I reckon sir that
Sometimes you can neva' get the boots on
Till you've worn em for a while. Boy's greener
Than a shoot of bluegrass. Ease up on 'im,
Then the men'll love y'a for't, much as I do,
General.

ANDREW JACKSON
(standing)

I accept your love, Sam, I do. But if
It came to you need's swaying on the rope,
Then the duty would be only more dear to me...

THE HANGING – MORNING

The wee wet boy stands on an old tin milkbucket a rough rope round his neck. Someone kicks. The boy kicks, kicks, kicks, sways. Andrew watches, stoic, situated on his horse.

ANDREW JACKSON
(reminiscing)

The execution was productive of the
Happiest effects, producing order, the fear
Of command and strict obedience, we were
Ready for the great trial of the campaign.

THE BATTLE OF HORSESHOE BEND – MARCH 27TH, 1814

Let every shot tell. The drum rolls and the charge. They scramble up the wall of the Indian fortress. Lemuel the first up through his forehead is driven a ball. Sam Houston next takes an arrow into his thigh yet fighting still, Crocket follows him up and over fighting. Come the others. Sharp knife Jackson mounts the wall riding his pale horse the whole fray below surveying he shouts commands all his blood is up flowing the fighting on into the night the Indians flee into the river – a squadron waiting on the other bank there – fire and light and the river runs red.

In the morning three hundred float like bloated rafts in the red water.

WILDERNESS OF TENNESSEE – EVENING

Baruni had fallen from Rachel. Afraid, her back all striped up, she'd ran away and her foot had tripped on a stone well that she did not see she fell onto the bramble and the brake.

BARUNI

(lamentingly)

I da' feet of my people, I run 'dem

Out of all da' mind chains 'dat were known,

Summoned to the sower's call, to walk the wine

Press all 'lone,

A grape vine runs Underground, hold da' stem,

And hoist ya'self to da' queenly North, climb

Dat long way up, like ladder of d'sunbem',

Where in da mouth is da' heavenly chime,

And sing and sing of da end of da Time.

Barefoot, wearing a straw-hat and overalls and a three-triangle stitch, SAHM.

SAHM

(singing)

'For I'se gwine home to Dina,

Yes, I am gwine home.

Den I ain't got time to tarry, I ain't got time to
dwell,

I'm bound t'de land a'freedom, o negros! fare y'a-

> *(stops; stands over her)*

Baruni, slave of Rachel, from where're you

Coming? Baruni, to where're you going?

BARUNI

I am running away the eyes of her.

SAHM

Carry yourself captive to Rachel, girl.

It's for yourself best down there in the South.

I've descendants to give to you down there,

Andrew's swelled your breasts with nursing, but
Sam'll

Swell your belly with birthing.

BARUNI

Who're you to

Talk? You're just a boy…

SAHM

I am SAHM all in all!

But you'll birth a boy! And you'll name him this,

'Ammon', for you've listened to your weeping

By your lady's lash, and I heard that too,

But soon you'll listen to your boy's crying

When out thy womb he falls!

BARUNI

Will I be pregnant but to property?

SAHM

Ammon will a rebel be, never none's

Property! A stubborn man! A wild one!

His guard up against them, a guard against

Them, their torches razing against him his

High pitched tents a light to all the ante-

Bellum bringing South, Ammon d'savior'll be.

BARUNI

You's a seeing Sam, I lived to see you,

So I'll call this well, Well Seen, it's between

Nashville and Memphis...

SAHM

(*blankly*)

Now git on going,

Back to y'a mistress, girl, or I'll tell.

BARUNI

Yes'sa.

She does as she said.

*So SAHM didn't tell the posse which was out houndin for
Baruni 'bout what he'd seen nor said. When they come on by,
he just whistles em right off.*

FORT JACKSON (HORSESHOE BEND) – DAY

William Weatherford the Red Stick Chieftain rides his coal
horse into the camp up to AJ lounging in the midst of his men.
The men they throw biscuit tins at the horseman and whistle.

> ANDREW JACKSON
> *(drinking brandy)*

And what do you want, sir?

> WILLIAM WEATHERFORD

> I am the head

Of Creek and Red Sticks. I come to surrender.

The laughter goes away.

> ANDREW JACKSON

Come inside, we'll talk there.

William dismounts. They go inside the fort.

> ANDREW JACKSON

I had ordered that you be brought in chains,

In ringing chains I'd have heard who you were.

> WILLIAM WEATHERFORD[1]
> *(in broken English)*

I'm in your power, do with me your power pleases

You. I have harmed the White all the harm I could.

---

[1] here follows a paraphrase of Commander Weatherford's
recorded words to the General

I fought them with all the fight I could, bravely and
Nobly. If I had an army of giants we'd contend to
The last. But we have only a field of our dead
Changing back to grass. My people, all ebb. Your
People, a wave growing. I can do nothing but water
My people with my weeping.

Look, I water the unfortunate grave of my nation.
Look, a man of war stands tall before you, but he
Can only weep and worry, and sigh and hunch over
The plot of his people, and groan and sigh, leaning
Back, forth, to and fro, in and out of the times,
Terms of his people. Then, I could animate air into
Their noses, my warriors, now, I exhale in vain,
I can't animate the dead to battle.

I sigh, and groan, lean in and out of the things I see.
I look into the present, miseries, misfortunes there,
Brought upon my country's head, a hail on their
Heads. I look farther, the coming times, the
Roughest sorrows coming this way, and I sigh and
Wish to warn it, the weeping trail, all backs a
Burden, all shoulders a trial, all their way, a way
Down, I wish to warn it, but I cannot ward it away,
No matter what I say. I sigh and lean out of the time
Of things again. I hold up my head, and I keep it up,

I weep no more. You are a brave man, I rely upon
Your generosity. You will exact no terms of a
Conquered people but that they can accede to.
But whatever they be, it would be madness
And folly to oppose your wish.

ANDREW JACKSON

The massacre at Fort Mims was not noble.

WILLIAM WEATHERFORD

That I did all I could do to dam, I could not dam all
The water of the anger, so the fort ran red like an
Iron river.

ANDREW JACKSON

You look White… Why did you lower yourself?

WILLIAM WEATHERFORD

What would have been mouths of the White to me,
Had I made the war cry with them against my men?

ANDREW JACKSON

You would have been called a traitor, to one instead
Of the other.

WILLIAM WEATHERFORD

In the woods beyond are all my women and
Children, I am a father of scores an' scores, for their
Fathers are in the earth again. Look, the women and
Children, they are like dry bones in the desert,
I plead for their mercy.

ANDREW JACKSON

Here are my terms, with them your wives, children,

Will live, without them, will be like their fathers.

Carry yourself captive to the far West.

It's for yourself best out there in the West.

You've descendants to give yourself out there,

Swell your tents with people, under protection

Of Amerika's steadfast hand and word.

Go back to your people, tell them these things.

WILLIAM WEATHERFORD

Yes, yes, war man, I can.

ANDREW JACKSON

Dear heart, you will…

He rides the coal horse out. They vanish West. They will not be invisible there forever.

WASHINGTON CITY – AUGUST 1814

The razing of the head City laid low. The redcoats they take its parts apart brick and mortar and coat in oil and set it a'flame. White City shining red on the hill in the night. The dull mumbling of distant cannon-fire. The White House red as a furnace for coals, and the burning lamps bled and then a tempest of the East a hurricane heaving, parting, razing the remnant walls, raising a soggy heap for the morning to see a heath for the owl and jackal, and the vermin live there.

ACT III

THE HERMITAGE – MIDDAY

Rachel holds Lyncoya's hand as he totters across the kitchen.
Baruni watches her.

RACHEL JACKSON
(to Baruni)

Now I do not expect capability

Of understanding the apparatus

On your part the science of cooling,

But the practicals I can teach for the

Benefit of the children and servants.

I'll unseal the mystery of heat to you

In just this way, and your domestic role

Will be fulfilled: Heat has its own power.

It moves by the touch. The air touches

The stove, is touching the flame, and that heats

It partner to partner along the air,

So we open windows in a way as

Though one could breath through, form a flue.

BARUNI

Yes ma'am.

RACHEL JACKSON
Now which windows would you open?

99

BARUNI

(walking across the dining room)

This one… and then ova' here, this one, mam.

RACHEL JACKSON

Yes and now we feel the breeze has its course.

Living in the master's house you'll mind the

Air at all times, but don't think that as I've

Taken you up out of the fields again

I'd as soon allow a breach of duty.

Now go into the pantry.

Baruni obeys, palming the beginnings of the bump of her breached womb, gathering the corn and the squash and the cabbage into a basket. Rachel (her large belly in bundles) also prepared the supper beside.

Andrew Jackson was napping on the porch in the midday heat, a glass of iced tea near his knee, a wide straw hat on his red (greying, greying) hedgy shock of hair.

SAHM was seen among the hickory and tall oak trees which Andrew had planted on the frontier of his plantation. Andrew opened his eyes: SAHM there on the edge with two older men.

SAHM seemed older maybe on the verge of twenty-four years old finely dressed like a gentleman standing plain as day on the field; fiery Andrew leaps up, runs out to meet him.

ANDREW

(prostrating)

SAHM! Don't pass your eyes over your servant.

The day's hot, the way ahead, is a long way,

There's water in the home, there's cool water

In the wells, well for me to wash your feet.

Rest under the middle oak that shades this place

A picnic, rest in shade of the day, I'll whim

To you, bringing the bread, water, and wine.

Let your journey wait. Let your passing o'er

Me be my gift, my hospitality.

Now SAHM spoke in tandem with his two men:

SAHM

(twining a lock of Spanish moss)

Place a picnic under the oak, but invite,

Into this area, your wife, her slave,

For we'd camp our words in their ears also.

*Andrew Jackson, he runs back to his home bursting through
the door stumbling into the kitchen plucking Lyncoya up
startling him tickling laughing with, breathless with-*

ANDREW JACKSON

O' happy day! Rachel! Baruni! Lyncoya!

Let no man say Sam's not blessed me! For here's

A family of many! We have guests

Hanging on under our oak tree! Listen,
Listen ye all, fashion ye our Southern
Hospitality in our south house
And port it out to the plain, for the Man
Divine, *that* he's grown up unto, waits out
There beneath us!

RACHEL JACKSON

       -Slow down, heart! Beat soft, heart,
And speak thy heat as the stove, controlled,
That we'd warm, not be bewildered by thee.

ANDREW JACKSON
(racing around the cabinets)

Decadent dishes! Out all the curtains
On our stash! Bring out quail, duck, smoked pork,
Pies, and the cornucopia, a feast
To make these pilgrims rich, harvests of squash,
Spinach, radish, potatoes sweet with browned
Sugar and unshell'd terrapins and unbeak'd
Canvasbacks, we'll invest a gumbo with
My Rachel's wild genius! Perch, catfish, trout,
Whitefish and shellfish beside the pears and
Peaches of thy fruit pie, the filling fills!
Baruni! What vegetables have stored we here?

BARUNI

Sir, we have turnips pickled in 'der jar,

Some spare asparagus sittin' a'spell,

A company of mandrakes ready for

Any order of the massa', and 'dis 'dat

I carry, a salad for any sir.

Andrew he laughs in delight lays Lyncoya in the basket of
greens in Baruni's arms kissing her quick on the lips running
up-stairs for his hickory cane, as Rachel went red as the
radishes. Andrew with his cane runs down and out—

ANDREW JACKSON

Hurry!

Into the yard he whistles loud and calls:

ANDREW JACKSON

Alfred! Alfred!

Alfred, a black boy, runs up.

ALFRED JACKSON
(clicking his heels; standing
at attention)

Aye, General! Here I am!

ANDREW JACKSON
(hands him a stone knife)

Take the motherless lamb you've tendered up

Into the cabin of blood, there butcher

Him. Bring the blessed parts to mistress Rachel.

ALFRED JACKSON

The lamb... You mean little Freddy?

ANDREW JACKSON

Little Freddy that's right, now get along, no lip.

AFLRED JACKSON
(teary eye'd)

No lip nor slip sir! I'll butcher the kid!

Aye! I won't think twice on edge of stone knife!

The stone's over the edge of thought, beyond

The point of mind! So no stone's sharp! So servant

Will be when his Massa gives him the lips

Of his hock'd order, order follows! Yes s'a!

When I go I dance, so's the joy of orderin'!

Alfred runs to the outfields looking for the lamb. He finds him in the shade of cedars on the bank of the creek far from the fields or the big house or the village of slanted huts where the slaves lived. Alfred sits with the lamb, brushing his curly coarse wool.

ALFRED

Well Freddy, Massa wants to eat you it seems.

But I'd not want to hurt you by any means.

You's just a lamb not knowing the world's why,

That you've been weaned but to labor and die,

Freddy, you've got a good life, you graze, roam,

Rest under whateva' tree 'dat sings to y'a,

You tastes all 'da grasses of 'da fine land,

Combining dat into your cud like a plug

Of black joy in my Massa's hand, but 'den

Da man 'dat gave thee life and bid thee feed,

All a sudden takes that life, bids it bleed,

Little lamb, O, little lamb,

We us both is called by 'dat name.

LIL FREDDY

Baaah! Baaah!

ALFRED

O Freddy! Freddy, I want Massa Andrew love me,

And see beneath 'dis my but sun-burnt face,

So I talks in 'da ways I can, turning

My words like the hairs of my head around,

That he'd neva' give me 'way nor sell me,

I know's you want 'dat for me too, Freddy,

All Massa wants is… just your warm black wool,

He's fixin' to make a warm winter blanket for us

Both outta' all dat curly hair you got dere', see,

You's white and pink unda'neath, so just let me

Shear you, 'das all I'm given to do, just shear you,

You'll be White again unda'neath-

-Cutting the throat with the stone knife. A jerking movement a blank voiceless shout betrayal and despair and if lambs could weep they would weep now in the arms of the black boy his friend. The boy weeps. The boy, red, takes the body to the

cabin on the edge of the third cotton field. Dresses it. The wool is sheared, piled, crimped into a fist, and held there hard in the fist.

Rachel bears the body angrily she prepares it by Baruni whom she strikes upon the ear for smiling for some unknown cause that is she suspects the cause of her infertility compared to her fertility and the contrast of the bump of her pregnancy in cutting contrast to her own bump of decadence.

Rachel, she gathers curds, milk, the lamb, her slave, her Indian ward; they meet Andrew on the porch.

They went down to SAHM. SAHM sits under the tree, his two older men, tycoons or planters, sitting beside. A moss mound and branch on the ground mounded by SAHM bored in waiting. He says nothing as they approach, watches with wide open eyes. Rachel picks the meal down for them under the tree. They stand over them, overseeing them eat. They ate.

SAHM
(chewing)

Your wife, Andrew, which one these's your wife?

RACHEL JACKSON

What fool question is that, dear sir!

ANDREW JACKSON

Rachel-

RACHEL JACKSON

-No, you're a guest here and you compare me
With my slave? Can't you tell easy which is
Which here, the mistress and the slave? Hm. Well,
I think you know mighty well who's who here,
And I'll show you your due Southern courtesy
When I say just as sweetly as I may I'm
The Mrs. Rachel Jackson and I'm most pleased
To make your acquaintance, *sir*, my husband's
Mentioned you much and with much compliment,
And gushing overestimatings of your
Courtesy, age, and your stature.

SAHM
(chewing, swallowing Freddy)

Rachel, you'll see a son rise in your womb,
When I appear again, it'll be mighty soon,
Your body will no longer be alone,
But by a boy's birth alone will you moan.

*Pause. The sound of the chewing of three curds. Rachel
laughs, her stomach hurting with the laughing, doubling
over, startling Andrew, Baruni, not SAHM.*

RACHEL JACKSON

Dear sir... Oh... forgive me, allow me a moment...
You're a young man, and I'll allow you some
Prerogative when you address the lady

Of the house, but this ignorance I cannot
Abide, why, boy, I'm older than two ya' mothers,
The bearing carriage has left the station,
Never to return, all my ticket's too late,
Ha! And husband, my coachman's goad is shrunk,
Does not harry the mighty steeds to race,
Their manes bald in age, their hooves un-shoed,
Young man, you know no doubt the groans of
    youth,
And think these the cliffs of passion, that in
Age these end, and only murmurs stoop o'er
Canes, chairs, and hobbled knees, but this' not so,
No, groans increase with the eld years' advance,
For all the sieges of life encroach the keep
To conduct sounds strange from the body aged,
Which combine on the besieged soul, no
Longer strong to stop the will of wishes,
To impregnate the impregnable with will,
So we groan for what's no longer able,
Like a frenzy for joust in a crippled King,
Who groans to lance the man, but can only
Pluck lyre string, I can't moan but bemoan this.

SAHM, his two men, had cleaned their face, and looked at
Rachel intently, then Andrew.

SAHM

Why does Rachel laugh? Is there anything
Too hard for SAHM? I won't be soft on you,
When I say something will be done, you'll do,
When the son starts to rise, I'll re-appear,
To Rachel a son, to Andrew an heir.

Lyncoya cries out in a sudden terror; Baruni takes him to her
bosom. Rachel looks on them, SAHM, blushes.

RACHEL

Forgive me sir, I did not laugh at you,
I was the subject of my shock is all.

SAHM

No, your stomach ached laughing, will ache again.

Slaves arrive carrying music, lay it before SAHM, which
stands.

ANDREW JACKSON

Can't you stay a moment longer with me?

SAHM

No. You have somewhere to go to.

ANDREW JACKSON

Send me.

A white mailman canters up to Andrew on his pony.

THE MESSENGER

'From the honorable Captain John Lafitte of

       Barataria,

To the most magnificent General of Amerika,

Andrew Jackson I a dire warning sling!

The British march upon New Orleans!

They will march into the streets! The Union Jack

Shall flap oer every door their wrath will pass over!

Behold! I occupy the river's mouth with many

Frigate, canon, and able seaman! In return for

Amnesty for my endless crimes of piracy,

I offer you my arm! Our defense of the city of

The seas will be an eternal acclaim! I want to be

A good sheep again, return me to thy sheepfold,

O leanest shepherd. Meet me at tavern Blind Mark!

Mark my words! ~Captain J. Lafitte.'

ANDREW JACKSON

By eternal, what is that darndest of all dross!?

THE MESSENGER

It's sent with sworn testimony from Governor

Claiborne, the message's true, the British move

To take New Orleans, then all the South thereafter.

Andrew looks, SAHM is gone. Rachel comes up to him.

RACHEL JACKSON

You must go, dear heart, walk again away

From me, and I'll be half our heart here.

110

ANDREW JACKSON

I won't leave you.

RACHEL JACKSON

              Know me tonight, unknow

Me in morning, we've promise to fullfill.

A child tonight, a nation in the morning.

Andrew he nods bends his head to her his heart.

NEW ORLEANS, A CABARET – SUNRISE, 1814

Three burlesque dancers smoke from long stems in the pink lounging after all the shows. Enter Ferdinando, swiping the pipe of one girl, Bijou, and smoking tailingly and she slaps him playfully on the thigh, (Fée and Nénette the other two).

BIJOU

Freddy! Honte à vous[1]!

FREDDY

              No show, Ms. Bijou,

Without a little smoke to hide the lines.

BIJOU

The show's tout over, Freddy, don't you know?

FREDDY

But I show's myself, Ms. Bijou, to you

---

[1] "shame on you"

And these vedettes[1] two, that are so fine after
The curtain falls.

He plants himself amongst the three girls.

FÉE

Oooh this old shell'd snail here's
Too slow don't you know.

NÉNETTE
(miming horns on her head)

Ou, c'est ca!

FREDDY

Snails take their time missus and missus oui.

BIJOU

And they're all slimy feet.
Sweep the floor, stoop and sweep it now, Freddy.

Down onto his hands and knees, he kneads the rug with palms.

FREDDY

Yes, Miss Bijou.

BIJOU
(putting her feet up on him)

There's a good nigger, Fred.

---

[1] stars; leading ladies

FREDDY

You's just as dark as me, Miss Bijou...

You three is the corner shades of the Night,

Your eyes the spring moons in that Night,

The hovers over the fields, a dawn, a dusk,

Oh show down on me, those pale eyes, show I toil.

NÉNETTE
(grabbing the riding crop)

Now you just keep toilin' in the earth, darky.

FREDDY

Yes Massa.

FÉE
(collaring him)

Looky, my pet snail, slug on.

FREDDY

Yes missus.

BIJOU
(leading him)

Now sing a spiritual.

FREDDY

I'll sing me out.

'You'd better run, run, run-a-run,

You'd better run, run run-a-run,

You'd better run to the city of refuge,

You'd better run, run, run!'

FÉE

Hehehe… now ride him like General Jackson's horse!

NÉNETTE

(saddling him)

Hehehe… Go on, git!

FREDDY

What's that you said bout General Jackson now?

BIJOU

We said git, horsey, go.

FREDDY

No, get off now.

NÉNETTE

We will horsey-

FREDDY

(standing roughly; then, pulling his collar off)

-Off! Off!

The ladies bunch up together in the corner.

FREDDY

How's you know bout General Jackson!? Tell Fred.

BIJOU

Why, he's here in New Orleans.

FREDDY

Why's he's here

In New Orleans?

BIJOU

Why for war he's the man.

NÉNETTE

The lobsta backs' comin to burn the town!

BIJOU

The Master's arriving this morning, Fred.

FÉE

Where you fleeing, Freddy?

NÉNETTE

Without payin???

Exit Ferdinando stiffly out the door into the red street.

NEW ORLEANS, PLACE DE ARMS, MORNING – 1814

City of noise, crescent city of curves, go down go down to you bayou plain marsh and bourbon rue and port of slavers and starboard slaves and gris gris[1] girls that strap the charms of sex on the necks. Andrew Jackson come, with swordfire, and martial lex. Go down, city, to see the General.

Andrew Jackson addresses all the city. First, the Whites:

ANDREW JACKSON

Albion[2] the oppressor of our infant

---

[1] A voodoo amulet
[2] Mythic giant which stands for England

Political existence, to contend

With which you have to contend, will be

To wax in power your national Power,

The revolution is not yet ended,

Whom yer pa's killed dead you must also kill dead.

For life, for liberty, for pursuit of joy!

The whites like grey'd carnations as they cheer in the carnage to come, hail the General. He appeals to the French:

ANDREW JACKSON

The English thy heel-clutching brother, invaded

That ward which you have adopted, and held

To your chest, this city thy femme, this femme

The Picts and Sax shall ravage and sack if

They your foes shall not face your righteous wrath!

Vive Liberté, Equalité, Fraternité! [1]

Polite applause. The cocking of guns the girding up of loins. The spittoons filling up. He talks to the Spanish:

ANDREW JACKSON

Remember the agonies of your brothers

Who nobly at Pensacola fought the foe,

Who just as nobly fell to the foe, rejoice,

Spaniards, that you might meet injury upon

---

[1] slogan of the French Revolution, 'Live, freedom, equality, brotherhood'

Injury on those that mar the name of Senor.

He talks down to the Blacks:

ANDREW JACKSON

Soldiers! From the Black Belt of the South I

Have rooted you up to arms. I invite

You to share in war as a man, to bear

His perils, to divide his glory…

To bind with us in bands of brotherhood,

I knowing you, knew that you could endure

All the hungers, thirsts, whips, and battle pangs

As well as the martial-est White stands here.

I knowing you, knew that you loved the nation

Of your nativity, that the patriot

Does not slumber in your dark hearts, but as

With a heart White, shall burn red when the time

Calls on you to defend the freedoms of men.

Even these expectations shall you surpass,

And grow to greater deeds, nobler qualities,

Which impels itself onward Amerikan.

Black hands hold the barrels of fire.[1] He to all the city:

ANDREW JACKSON

Now all cry Liberty! And march to meet

---

[1] Jackson, to much controversy, had armed the slaves
of the area to fight the coming British army

The Giant of England, build up the walls
Of our Holy Mountain Amerikan,
Our edges shall end him, and shall long live
This land of endless Life!

Cheers for Jackson.

THE EDGES OF NEW ORLEANS –
DECEMBER 23, 1814

Redcoats came down through that country like a hurricane. They followed the canals south to the Great River. They stepped the swampy marsh, through orange and black diamondbacks, the ancient alligator, the mosquito air, the airy forests of river cane, to the edges of the plantations.

They break into big houses they rough and tie up Black and White together. They burn black the crops and cane and houses that have not the Union Jack above the door. A black sun in a noon day. The air is sweet with the sugar. Gabriel, a slave, runs to New Orleans to Andrew Jackson laid up in bed with shaking[1].

---

[1] Jackson faced injury and illnesses almost
constantly, of the bullet in his shoulder and intestinal
diseases most especially

GABRIEL

The British are coming! Eight thousand strong!

Within six miles of the city the Beast

Of the East hunches in his dark den!

Cry panic! Let the women and children

Be let out to run! Flee! Flee all! Flee now!

There was much fear in the city that night. They bury their money under the house, sink their jewelry in the swamp. Andrew Jackson, he rides through the streets on his horse, shouting.

ANDREW JACKSON

Do not be alarmed, New Orleans! Sois calme!

Estate calmado! The enemy will not sleep on our

Soil until they lie dead!

The enemy will not reach the city! Hear all!

Amerika is able to defend!

He rides through the night, past Ferdinando, who stands in a green doorway, wide eye'd. The British artillery the city.

It is a conflagration, a sight to see.

THE BOMBED-OUT APARTMENT OF
ANDREW JACKSON – MORNING

Pirate Jean Lafitte and his band of brigands saunter up to
Andrew and his lieutenants. Jean wears a red frock'd coat,
black boots like hooves, and a gaudily feathered hat.

JEAN LAFITTE

Hail Andrew King! All hail Andrew King!

ANDREW JACKSON

Arrest that man.

JEAN LAFITTE
(draws his cutlass)

Nay, stay! I'll make a mince

Of a man that bars me from serving

Andrew Jackson, even Andrew Jackson! Stay!

Jean Lafitte shall swear to you his arms and feet!

With a wave of his hand, Andrew backs down his men.

ANDREW JACKSON

So this' the brigand clumsy pirate that letter'd me.

JEAN LAFITTE

Pirate!? Bonjou[1]! I am a privateer!

I demand satisfaction! Swin-twa!

---

[1] "hello!"

ANDREW JACKSON

I decline your demand to duel, as I've

Another engagement on the morrow.

His men, they laugh.

JEAN LAFITTE

Cila qui rit vendredi va pleure dimanche[1]!

You laugh at Lafitte? Lafitte laughs at you. Ha!

New Orleans is more than a mere morrow,

She's the city of sounds; all that passes

Through her many ears 'est like her rivers' wealth!

Dilo toujou couri larivière[2]!

You and all your host, c'est no more than 'Pop'!

And the city will hear of you no again, for

She's too busy hearin the next men, Andrew.

ANDREW JACKSON

If I didn't need your galleons, I'd hang you.

JEAN LAFITTE

Oh! Chien jappo li pas morde[3]! But Jean, he

Is an Amerikan!

ANDREW JACKSON

You, Amerikan!?

---

[1] "he who laughs on Friday will cry on Sunday"
[2] "water still runs the river"
[3] "the barking dog does not bite"

JEAN LAFITTE

Oui! O monsieur how Jean wept when White House

Burned down black! Oh, all the labors of Sam up

In smoke! Désolé! Despair! But Sam's a wise

Young man! He appoints his big man Andrew

To re-build the sucker, a new White House,

A new sky, a new land! Let him measure

The pattern: I saw da'White city of heav'n

Fall aside Potomac, and the measure

Of it was five hundred cubits square!

And a tall wall was around the White House,

Six cubits thick! And a raised platform high!

And all was walls all the way in, layers

Of Holiness 'til innermost oval

Completed the organism of her oui!

Satisfaction! May I slap your face, sir?

ANDREW JACKSON

No. I'm ill with the gout, with dysentery,

I'm holding two bullets in this old flesh;

I can barely sit up in my horse, sir,

I give orders to men from the head of my bed, and

I've a battle with the Britannic Power,

Outnumbered, outgunned, it'd be easy to

Be overrun on any attack from any side

And I must rely on a population

That is neither Amerikan nor

Any else other than New Orlean. And on

Them do I stake the fate of a country

Barely born, a country I'd create, which

Like the father, relies on the rising

Of the son, and I bear this weight, burdens

Of vision and will, without a whimper,

Nor a grimace nor curse nor complaint,

But even I, by the Eternal, would

Not withstand the power of your hand, Jean.

Jean tilts his hat'd head far back to chuckle and guffaw.

JEAN LAFITTE

Monsieur! Mo linm twa[1]! I love you!

Di moin qui vous laimein, ma di vous qui vous ye[2]!

The pig knows well on which wood it'll rub!

Hehehe. Cochon conne sir qui bois l'apé frotte[3]!

ANDREW JACKSON

Now come inside. We've a battle to win.

The British are arranged in the field a 'face the city. The city is facing them back, walled and manned. Jean and his fleet

---

[1] "you are my twin"
[2] "tell me who you love, you tell me who you are"
[3] "the hog knows on which wood he rubs"

hold the waterways. The British drag their groaning cannons through the mud. The city waits. They are face to face.

A NEW ORLEANS NIGHT – JAN. 8TH, 1814

The red doors shut the windows barred the beads the jewelry buried, or sunk in the alligator's mouth. Caterwauling of cats. A work of a last shudder après mort. Death's head jokes around the bivouacs. Andrew drifted the battlements a hand on a shoulder of a boy or a man each a son of a familial war.

Voodoo. Hoodoo. Some are wrapped in red flannel around the neck some clutching tarot decks to the breast. The Hanged Man's face up (in upsides, down). The card of dancing fools. All are afraid. They squat and sweat. All are black in the night.

There are Songs down Queen Laveau Street. Andrew angry (the infraction of the curfew on sound) hounds it down alone.

THE SINGING
(with beat and drum)

Great spir't o' mine!

Great spir't o' mine!

O God Zimbi!

Great spir't o' mine!

Great spir't o' mine!

Papa Zimbi!

My li'l boat,

Is now standing still

And, can't cross the bay,

O, I wonder, Great spir't o' mine,

What can it be!

What can it be!

O'![1]

The narrow alleys. The surprising corners turn to see a green lantern above a green door. The song, the African voices, the African drums and feet thumping like a thousand hearts under a sternum. Andrew opens the door:

SAHM grinning there leaps up running out into the night, running in step shouting song. Andrew, he's led by the ear.

ANDREW

Wait for me ahead! Make no noise! No noise!

SAHM[2]
(singing; running)

Adya Houn'to, drumming vodun, shall play

On the palms the meaning of the life-show,

---

[1] Great Spirit O' Mine, translated by Werner Jaegerhuber, a song indicative of voodoo

[2] a series of invocations to voodoo deities

125

Draw from the deck the Magus trump, enchant

This hour of midnight's middle by Me in midst,

I will show you our perseverance in the black soil,

For the footprint of Congo's on all these

Cobblestones he's the indefinite White

Throat of the man-eater prowling the night,

Swallow us now thou sexfull 15th devil,

Leaning out of that manhole with that doll

Pierced by the fifteen needles and I'll flee

In to an other man, you'll not slave me

In all an'all, Congo, for I hear the gag

Of big Bondye's red throat: Damballa,

Wedo serpent, thy seven thousand coils

Shall capace all creation, thou enfacer,

Thou who enfaces thyself upon the draws

Of random decks of an Arcana moon…

O' Dambala, come Dambala, on the

Seventh day, remain in the grave, and turn,

Turn to seven thousand worms slavers

That eat on the body, black Body, wish

For the augury, of Man turning to

Turnity. Shakpana! Shakpana! Pox on me thy

Small yet numerous hills and I will be

The landscape.

Lay on this giant table of me the

Card of Lovers. Mate me made with the Man

Or the Woman who is the Amerikan

And the Aggassou we interbreed!

SAHM runs up onto the stage. Andrew follows him there. A
third man bars him, wearing a black tail'd coat, palming his
elaborate ivory cane, drinking his 21 lumps of sugar in the
sweet-sour, Baron La Croix, parts his lips and hisses out:

BARON LA CROIX
(happy from ear to ear)

Death's the punchline of life!

A gag in the stab of a knife!

Like crying over a bee-sting,

All da' woe comes to naught a'thing!

SAHM
(soliloquizing on stage)

Will I to Andrew be a mystery?

What will I will? Andrew must still issue

A great Nation between those long, thin legs,

Pushing a populous from his person.

On a night, I knew him within, he's full,

He'll pour out passion for SAHM on all the land,

Follow the Amerikan way: Justice,

Freedom, Liberty, and leaning on Other,

The sep' States, united to SAHM's sound word.

But the noise of New Orleans rises up,

All their contempt of me, growing up to me,

Makes heavy this heart, a sinking heart

Shall fall down to its pull, I will go down

To see this city, and I'll bring it down if

It brings me down any lower I'll lower it,

So in razing I'll raise it and be pleased

To start anew. My Baron La Croix shall

Bring the roach and the worm and the black crow

To the tabernacle of the war corpse,

And they shall go forth, and look upon the

Worms that dare not die, among corpses do

Not dust, the fire that shall not cease, then

Shall all flesh fear a citizen of SAHM.

SAHM descends the stage, down towards the city, down to kill. Andrew, he faces him, standing in his way. La Croix quickly cracks his head. Andrew into darkness a dreamless.

THE SECOND DREAM OF ANDREW JACKSON – NIGHT FOR DAY

Andrew, SAHM, walking side by side down the wall of the city, together on the wall, while the British army, there on the field, are like an ocean waving towards New Orleans, like thick clouds, darkness and deep, pale lighting and hectic red.

ANDREW
(holding his hand)

Will you wipe out Orleans' innocents? Those

With contempt for you, the Blacks, foreigners,

See, they stand beside us just as ready

To water red thy tree of Liberty,

What if fifty patriot men this city defend,

Can Sam not hold himself back for them?

Shall the Executive of all the World

And Country and Legislator of all

Our Laws, not be lawful now? Shall the Judge

Not be judicial in this case?

Thunder, the cannon the eighteen pounder the four twenty-four-point carronades dragged through mudmuck shall relieve a fire on the city, the spilling of anger on the city.

SAHM

If fifty patriots for New Orleans bleed,

I will hold back my ire.

Night, & the Amerikans & Orleanians sneak to flee the fight or to murder with flintlocks & knives the red men camped 'round the pitched fires or walking alone in the dark.

Andrew Jackson, SAHM, they among the camp of the British like phantoms:

ANDREW
(shoulder to shoulder)

Listen to me, listen to me, I've dared

To imagine you may speak to me, Sam,

I who am but a breathed red clay, am not

Afraid to move urges unto thy ear,

What if forty patriots defend?

The fog drapes the morning, cannon in the rising fog, the red men through the forest step lightly and carefully their way-

DAVY CROCKETT
(red)

-Fire! Fire!

Andrew, SAHM, wandering among the trees the falling men autumn'ing like aimless aiméd leaves.

SAHM

Then I will not pull them down to the ground.

ANDREW

Please, Sam, keep your patience with your servant,

What if thirty patriots defend New Orleans?

Now they come like the flood up the field all the columns of the Red in thick formations to her frontal assault lobstereds on the march, on their own backs they climb, over the ditches over their own dead up the ladderless ditch, cutting down, being cut down, along the up, drowning in the scumb'd of the ditch, or trampled, or dying by fire or dying by the sword.

SAHM

For thirty I will not wipe away the

Living with the dead.

Andrew examines the face horrorstuck that stares on heaven that suffocated in the stamp of boots of earth. He pulls SAHM down to him, pressing him close, bare chest to bared chest.

ANDREW

What if twenty true blooded Amerikans

For this city of thousand sounds shall bleed?

A struggle for a hill of mud that changes bloody hands. The hill is theirs or then theirs or they that come up and over the wall of New Orleans or they that tumble down its nether side, and are butchered at the bottom.

Look, those that cross the river, are swallowed by the cannons of galleons, and roll back into river. One General, I don't know which side, shall mount up and fall, his army retreat, turning the red tide, their backs blown down by giant lungs, their backs to them, plungingly they go down.

SAHM

I will not pull down all for that twenty

That stand tall, their backs straight, every inch

Of them an Amerikan.

By SAHM, so it was.

In morning, the thousand left dead plant the field like flowers red. The Amerikans, Orleanians, British, they walk out on the ceasefire, wander the garden, mourn or rejoice, depending on the recognition of the culture planted there.

Andrew, SAHM, stroll the garden in the cool morning, hand in hand and leg to leg, they stand by two Amerikans who pluck and toss three unidentifiable, into the soiled ditch.

                      AN AMERIKAN GRAVEDIGGER
                  (smoking; cajoling
                  a British prisoner)

Nine hundred and thirty-three plus these two makes
Nine hundred and thirty-six redcoats coated in the
Black blankets of their bed. Did you hear whatta
Said? You wicked Brit. Know how many
Amerikans take the long nap? Not more than eight!
Only eight eat the dirt fattenin' for their worms
That's to nine hundred and ninety nine Reds to
Eight Free men, that's an arrangement I like I do.
Did you hear me, Brit? Look on that man in the
Hole, there's a thousand other of em just like him in
The hole and you'll be there too, Brit, you'll be
There too your life flows from you from the cannon

Leg, look, you water yer own plot with that weepin.

Andrew, SAHM, face to face.

ANDREW

Eight.

SAHM

Lastly, I will not burn them for eight.

SAHM had finished speaking.

He turned, separate from Andrew, and walked further down the countryside, whistling. Andrew, he turned, separate from SAHM, and walked up into the city, his side, silent.

Enter, Ferdinando. He sees the body of a black man.

FREDDY

Black be any skin that sees.

A body's red as the rest, in its rest,

Here's Master's will in address: you grow here,

You there, make for my maggots, changing hills,

To be such a planter of man's the best. Not planted.

He goes back into the city. From afar, he sees Andrew in the crowded marketplace, where Andrew is lauded by all alike.

FERDINANDO
(to Andrew; whispering)

We is Massas both, brothers by the bond,

Come, let's not quarrel ova' white bones.

So this New Orleans' saved, and now yous can

Yourself go, face the whole country, and make

Your own Amerika, Fredy'll not butt in,

Freddy'll let Andrew Jackson go,

But remember that by us blacks it was so.

Madly, he struts around as on a horse.

FERDINANDO
(as Andrew Jackson)

They bled as red as the rest. So

Further south go, Ferdinando.

He goes.

The war for Amerika won. The British went back across the Atlantic, never to return. Bodies were buried or burned. Prisoners returned to their places. Blacks go back to their handlers; their hands hold no firearms. A parade in the city of New Orleans in the noiseful morning. Rachel Jackson struts, hand in hand with Andrew, through the parade.

NEW ORLEANS
(singing)

Hail to the Chief! Who hied at war's alarms,

To save our threatened land from hostile arms!

Jackson, all hail! Our country's pride and boast,

Who's mind's a council, and who's arm's a host!

Remembrance long shall keep thy fame,

And future infants learn to lisp thy name!

Now sing a song for Sam!

A loud shout that's grand!

A song we wrote when the night was darkest,

When the British sat on us all their weight,

Just hear this one, it was all worth the wait!

O' say, can you see,

By the dawn's early light,

What so proudly we hailed,

At the twilight's last gleaming?

Whose broad stripes and bright stars

Through the perilous fight,

O'er the ramparts we watched,

Were so gallantly streaming?

And the rocket's red glare,

The bombs bursting in air,

Gave proof through the night,

That our flag was still there,

Oh say, does that star-spangled banner yet wave

O'er the land of the free and the home of the brave!

Andrew, Rachel, they ride out, hailed everywhere they went.

THE AMERIKAN PEOPLE

When'll General Jackson for President run?

Himself he's conquered, and our war he's won!

The People carry him home like a crown. Andrew, he lays down, weary, in his own bed. He dreams of the Presidency.

Iostaf, small as a thumb, stands up over his snoring bedhead.

IOSTAF
(*aside*)

While my leviathan sleeps, a minnow grows,

Which on his dread back's sucked to swim further,

Aye, I'll my Ferdinando the 2nd show, no nurther.

THE NEGRO FORT,
APALACHICOLA RIVER, FLORIDA –
1816 [1]

Freddy was walking through the farms and fields which the Africans had shaped tilled and irrigated by the river. He was hello'ing his neighbors, sucking in free air with greed and humming out crude new tunes.

FREDDY
(*singing as he strolls*)
'O Zip a duden duden duden zip a duden day.

O Zip a duden duden duden duden day.

---

[1] The Negro Fort was built by the British to assist in
an attack from the south during the War of 1812.
When Jackson ensured the surrender of the British, it
became occupied by renegade and armed African
Americans, provocatives to the slave-holding South

O Zip a duden duden duden zip a duden day.

Zip a duden duden duden zip a duden day.'[1]

He strolls by Betty's bungalow; she is young and black and has been lashed seven times for three escape attempts from her chattel prostitution.

BETTY

Morning Freddy!

FREDDY

Morning Betty! Good day!

BETTY

You goin up to da fort now, Freddy?

FREDDY

Yes mam! Gonna make sure them young boys up
There is got their heads on straight still, yes mam!

BETTY

You let 'em be, Freddy!

FREDDY

(strolling; singing)

'O ist old Suky blue skin, she is in lub wid me

I went the udder arter noon to take a dish ob tea;

What do you tink now, Suky hab for supper,

Why chicken foot an posum heel, widout any

---

[1] 'Zip Coon', in the version by George Washington
Dixon. Freddy's singing predates the actual writing
of this problematic, historical, American minstrel

137

butter!'

Tom lumbers along aside. He is big, tall, broad. Blood is dry
on his hands, by the beheading and plucking of chickens.

TOM
(carrying gun, a shovel,
one on each shoulder)

What song is that you's singing, Old Freddy?

FREDDY

Don't know! Just making it up as I go!

The words bubble up in the night like some

Sweet stew my mammy used to make in her

Seer' cabin after I's got done serving

Up the big house. Why, I'd get words all the

Time in the night, and I didn't like the words

That'd come at first, I thought they was mean words

That meant no good, but the noise got so bright,

Shinin' the times, I took shinin' to them,

Shining to that dark dark thangs, took da rangs,

Prett' soon, polished em to a sheen, den done

Shackle'd em to a tune, now them I do sing!

I can't stop! I can't not dance nor skip neither!

Dese' here knightly lands make minstrelsy to me!

TOM

I can't say I'm taking a shining to

That now, Freddy. You's an old'ing man.

138

The sun's baked you too black and bald, and what

Hair you have there is straight white. Good day.

Exit, Tom to dig a canal. Freddy hopped up into the Fort,
which is bleak grey stone with lively banners waving
runaways in.

FREDDY
(chorus)

'I went down to Sandy Hollar t'other arternoon

A' first man I chanced to meet war ole Zip Coon;

Ole Zip Coon he is a natty scholar,

For he plays upon de Banjo "Cooney in de hollar!'

Tall thin Prince storms into his face his cutlass on his hip.

PRINCE

Shut that trap up now, old Freddy!

FREDDY

Yes'sa.

Massa Prince, ya'll headin to the pow-wow now?

PRINCE

I ain't your 'Massa' nor anyone else's,

Old Fred, I done told you that many times.

FREDDY

Massa's in da blood, sa'. Just because you's

Black that don't mean you ain't got it in y'a,

And I's got the same blood, but it flows the

Otha' way round, so I's a servant see,

Always has been, in da Big Houses, now here

In da Nigga Fort, ifn' it please

Y'a sir, I'd like to sit in on da big talk.

PRINCE

> (*disgust*)

Long's you ain't lending to 'da big talk' I'll

Allow it, old 'servant' Freddy; I 'spect

All this freedom's fried you, such fol-de rol[1],

Mm mhm, no. It is unmanly…

*They go into the keep. There, around a table: Garçon, 30
years old, the leader, a former slave to the Spanish. Cyrus, a
free man, a carpenter. There is a Choctaw Chief and his
trusted men. There are several black men one black woman
nursing two babes, and there is a black boy, Pip, giving
crumby coffee corn & found rations.*

GARÇON

Now you tell me quick how it went down, boy.

AN AFRICAN FUGITIVE

> (*wounded, hoarse voice*)

We was up the riva', way up the riva',

Two displaced Creeks was there runnin' wid us

Up the way, and they was the ones that saw

---

[1] gaudy nonsense

The white flashes of the White shimmerin
In the water, between the reeds of slough
And marsh, they was naked, two, like dem
Old ancensta's, but these was two Amerikan
Naked as the day they broke their way
Into our world. They was bathing. Then the
Third came, clothed, clothed them, took 'em two,
Further down riva', we followed em, they drank
From the stream, as we lay on our bellies,
Mouth down in all that water. We listened to
Their talk. We listened to their mean, vain talk
As on us Nature slithered or swam
Heedless of our fugitive heads.

GARÇON

And what did they say?

CYRUS

Some worst wicked words...

AN AFRICAN FUGITIVE

Aye that's as you said, they said, so it was.
They'd come down from Fort Scott, drawing water
For all them White's up there in their fort, they'd
Come down hunting for us, 'Ol Nigger Fort',
They said they was gonna sniff out us 'coons'
And put down all us raging, rabid rabble,
And dog the rest us back to our 'Masters',

Where they would whip us wicked for willing.

CYRUS

And the water did boil,

For rage at bondage of their wives and babes

And men re-made to slaves!

AN AFRICAN FUGITIVE

Aye sa', we made geysers and clouds of steam,

Like men in the rivers of Hell,

Ragefull we rose from the slough, riva'stones

Fitt'd to our palms, bellowing sum war whoops

I ain't neva' knew we knew, and the White

Went paler than I eva' thought they could,

As on them our rage fell, as da riva' ran red...

But one of them devils we took alive.

FREDDY

Lord! Lord! Forgive 'em! Oh Lawd! Dear Lawd!

PRINCE

Hush! Old coot!

GARÇON

Peace! This prisoner, where's he?

CYRUS

In the powder keg. He's done bust his leg,

We'd could carry him out to y'a, rack'd on

His stretcher, and whip him up.

FREDDY

Awe Lawd help dat man!

GARÇON

Bring him in to us.

Exit, Cyrus. Freddy slaps his own balding head, repeatedly, groaning, fearing Sahm.

FREDDY

You'll invoke Sam down on all our poor heads

You harm a hair of that White man's crown.

PRINCE

Already kill't two em devils, old coot.

Afraid, Pip runs out the tower and the town, to the sea. The Amerikan is brought in, bloodied burnt & battered. Silence settles over all, except the whimpering of Freddy crouching in the corner. Garçon leans over the Amerikan, lifts his head.

GARÇON

How many coming down from Fort Scott, boy?

THE WHITE AMERIKAN

Ha! Ah! N-n-nigger-

He's struck.

FREDDY

-No sa'! Don't hit him 'gain!

143

GARÇON

Cyrus, take him outside, tie'im to the stretcher.

So it was done: the Amerikan is tied in the center of the fort,
supine, splayed for all to see.

GARÇON

Pour the oil on him.

THE AMERIKAN

No! No, God! Please please please!

Prince, the lamp of the oil in hands, pours the unction on the
head of the man who moans and sputters. The oil anoints the
man. They strike in a flame and set it on a wick.

CYRUS

The flame of rage shall unbound, from the bound,
Will burn to binder, union in da' fire.

A WOMAN

Don't do it. Don't y'all burn this man!

Cyrus hands the burning lamp to Prince who approaches the
man who moans howls screams.

Look, Freddy steps in, lays himself on the man.

FREDDY

I won't let ya's do this, young man, no sa'!

PRINCE

Move, old fool.

144

FREDDY

No, you's got to burn me too.

I can lay here's long as I like-

A WOMAN (2)

-For a White man!?

AN AFRICAN MAN

He's quadroon, he's quit his half's heritage's why.

PRINCE

He's worse, he's a house nigger. He got their blood

In his head too, we should burn em both then,

They a twins two.

GARÇON

No! No... Douse that lamp, Prince.

PRINCE

But sa'!

GARÇON

Douse it!

And now bring that White man back to the keg.

Freddy? You hear that? You's can get up now.

Ol' Whitey's gonna be alright. Now listen

All y'all, the White man's coming for us, cuz

Any time a Black rise anywhere, White's

Gotta come to cut him. I don't know how much

There'll be, but we've got arms, armor, and canon

Here, and a fort's formed to defend. So we'll

Make a defense of it good. Bring in your
Women and children to the keep. You men,
Gird up your teeth for a good fight. Git on!

All was done as he said.

THE NEGRO FORT – MIDDAY

A few days later, Freddy was outside the gate napping in the midday heat, brandy by his knee, straw hat over his balding and curling white hair, when two of SAHM's were seen among tall oak trees which curled their moss melancholy above the brook.

Freddy opened his eyes: two of SAHM's there on the edge, two older men arriving like auctioneers they chew their plugs approach & bow & doff their hats.

FREDDY

Hear me, Massa's, stop at my house. Stay the
Impending night. I'll wash your feet with some
Riva' water, then you can run refreshed
In the morning. Don't go into the fort.
It can wait a day more, good Massa's, wait.

SAHM'S

No, Jim, we'll pitch by the road to picnic.

146

Freddy, he begs them, fawning charming catching. The two men, they stop for him, go up into his cabin by the river, eat there. The Africans, they see them, come to Freddy's door.

PRINCE
(knocking, knocking, knocking)

Freddy? Freddy!? Who have you got in there!?

Night. All from old to young press round the cabin their stiff guns bucking in their yearning arms.

CYRUS

I saw them two men, slave traders inside

Inciting us, flesh fairs, the sunder'ers

Of mothers and their children, of husbands

And our women to the deep darkening of

Our hearts, the scream coloring of

Our skins, O wicked back of men. Freddy's foul.

ALL OF THEM

Where are your two men, Fred? Bring them out of

There for us. We want to know what they're made

of.

We want to know them for their blood. Let's see

red.

FREDDY
(at the door; trembling voice)

Don't ring the rage of Sam! These is my guests,

These two Southern gentlemen, they's come down

From far, far up. Don't show your anger. Swallow

It up, you young men, swallow that rage into dark,

A darky dances anger out of his meek grin, o Lawd,

You can whip me instead if you want.

Leave the gentlemen unda' my roof unhandled.

THEM ALL
(breaking down the door)

Get out of our way, Uncle Fred.

FREDDY

No! Lawd!

A hand brought Freddy back to SAHM. He holds him. Flash!
Firecrackers burst and bang like rockets out the door.
Blinding the eyes. Bang! They grope and fawn for the door.

Out in the fields, Freddy and SAHM.

SAHM'S

If you've got family you'd like to take, Jim,

Now's the time to harvest 'em. The threshing

A-gonna-come down on the nigger fort

For its offense offends us SAHM, sends us

To bring low the rising of the Negro.

Ferdinando goes, door to door begging everyone he knows
to leave. He prophesies. They laugh. Old man mad man. He
begs until the dawn.

SAHM's, they bring Freddy holding the hands of two mulatto
girls he'd stolen out away from the fort. He's scared, resists
the pull.

SAHM'S

The fort is foul with a tempting contempt,

Nor boy nor girl nor babe from us' exempt,

So dance out the way, old Jim Crow[1],

Save that cursed skin and watch the show.

Ferdinando, he weeps moans and howls, he is taken holding
the stolen girls out the way of the Fort. He's over the river.
Thunder, on the horizon rolling, gunboats, men approaching.

SAHM

Ferdinando, into the swamp!

FREDDY

Sa', charity on me, sa', I'm an old

Old man, I've got nothin in all the world,

And these two stray girls is got even less,

Keep your servant in the land of the livin',

The slough and swamp's a march of the dead, sa',

I'm branded to any Amerikan niggers

Might meet me, U T, that's what's writ on me,

I tempt their contempt. Let's instead

---

[1] it's unknown when the folk-figure, 'Jim Crow',
began, but his infectiousness has not abated

Enslave ourselves again, o sa', there's fine

Little Spanish plantation not far from here

Called 'Poco Azúcar', is a little place sa',

We'll be little there, little to the end of Life.

SAHM

Hm, I do pity the darky, so I'll

Not level the plantation, Spanish though't be,

Since you speak for it, very well Ol' Tom,

Fly to plantation! Imprison yourself there,

In serving, earning peace, till term of you.

Freddy, his two girls, they run to Poco Azúcar through the incredible darkness as

The sun dawns like a spearpoint raising in the sky. And

The Amerikans in the river rise up to the fort, surround it. In the hold of the gunboats, SAHM crouching, grinning there.

ACT IV

THE NEGRO FORT – JULY 27TH, 1816

THE AMERIKANS

Surrender! Submit! Lower yourselves, come down
From up there, or we'll level you from down here!

Garçon hoists the Union Jack high over the fort. He waves it in the wind. The Africans cheer, cajole, chant the Royal Anthem.

GARÇON

We are men and women. We'll only kneel
To a country that knows us as we are!

THE AMERIKANS

Let your women and children out, return
Them, and we'll have our duel.

PRINCE

Live free or die!

CYRUS

Better buried than bonded!

GARÇON

Fire the canons! Fire the guns! Fire fall down!

They miss every shot. The return volleys ricochet off the fort.
SAHM is in the hold of the boat, loads the hotshot into the
canon's mouth, aims it heaven high the shot flies over the fort
and falls like a meteor into the powder kegs.

White light. A sound too loud for the ear to contain tons.

The fort, it's overturned laid low leveled a sad heap under a
plume of heated black smoke. Ash. The space undone. All the
agriculture around burns the cabins the charred skeletons of
what they were before. A little hill of salt on the black ground.

270. 270. The Amerikans come off their boats and see the
face of the thing:

The bodies that hang in the trees the parts of bodies boughed
in branches, the dust on the ground or under scattered stones,
jawbones and the thigh embedded upright like rites in the
ground, the wrong red, of ash, flames, blood and

The little ones, that hang from pines in stripes, in strange.

The Amerikans, some vomit, some feel fine.

Look, Garçon is hauled out from under a great red rock.
Garçon, of a weary people, his legs broken, he cannot walk
or stand, his face is white, but only with ash.

THE AMERIKANS

You had an Amerikan prisoner. You kill him?

GARÇON

(blind; hoarse)

We put him in the powder room. O' my

Enemy, you done burned him black with the

Rest of us, and the oiled and anointed

Became the fire, when the fire they met, on

Their weary way outta Hell. Hallelujah.

O' my enemy, each of us you stomp

Widens the wine of the Lord, the press of

The vintage, She'll drink on the day of Her,

On the day of Her, Her mountain descend,

Mountain level the land, Her's is a Holy Mountain,

She is in our midst, you men. You've refined

Her revealed, you wickedest of White men.

In my blindness, Her sight, in sighs, her ears,

She's thumping her breast she's shouting out voice:

'And these tears shall be shed no more for my

Children on the day of Me, when the floods

Of fire shall refine the country clean, when only,

Crisp apples, shall hang from our trees,

An' sweet sounds, scents, shall cling to the breeze,

Even the little ones, black lambs, shall be at ease,

Though they lie down beside a White man, no
Fear shall be in them. No fear. No fear. She's said.
'It is done even now', She say.

They give his body to the Creek who shoot him promptly into the head and they scalp the head and they loot the corpse of the fort, as this was the bargain for which the warpath went.

The Choctaw Chief, pulled out of the wreck, head of many men, his scalp is left to dry in the wind on the pole that stood crooked on the shattered ground. The Africans, a few survived, what is left of them, are re-enslaved.

And an Andrew Jackson, the next morning, arrives arisen on his pale horse and looks down on the fort glow like a low burning coal, its smoke producing and pushing a profound blackness up that mingles into air.

Here on the place was renamed, is known to this very day as:

FORT GADSEN, IN AMERIKAN
FLORIDA – MONTAGE

Andrew Jackson made sorties outward from there and conquered the land of Florida. Blacks go back into bondage. Indians, who'd scalped women and children, go to the gallows.

The steamboat, the cotton gin. This drove industry down South, Amerikans down South. The South was filling with people, flowing with wealth and chattel, flowing like the Mississippi River.

Andrew Jackson becomes Governor of Florida. Look, Rachel lies with him in his mansion by the sea. They comb the beach. Empty seashells. Drifting debris. The call & curse of the surf.

POCO AZÚCAR – DAWN

There the moon hangs pale in an azure mount. In blue shadows, Freddy, his two stolen girls, run off the plantation, for the Masters had beaten him bad & the Slaves they'd scorned him. His mouth is full of salt. Through the thickets of marked sugar canes, into the swamp, to the edge. Dismal. There is a small cave in the cliffside. They go in, hide there.

Cramped as a rattletrap, a cache of spirits is stowed – with wine whiskey grog and port firearms chains manacles spiked collars and an all's sold auction bill – in the slave catcher's cave.

Freddy, the two girls, they drink. The blood hounds' howl echoes as through a well. Days pass, in fear and the drinking.

FREDDY

(examining the spike collar;
in drunkenness)

Aviary of the heavenward mind,

Da' crows will fly not far from this ol' roost,

So's we's keep them wings clipped to earth, I say

We's cuz that's my duty, girls, ear to Ol'

Freddy, it was his duty to encollar

The running negroes of the field, I 'member

Each one, they'd have nails up towards the soft

Flesh of d'neck, even when they was bowing

To us they'd prick themselves with spots of red,

Lines of red, tricking on the black back down,

Collars'd have bars go way up ova' the head,

All the way round, he's couldn't lie down to sleep,

Nor eat nor speak nor kiss nor spit nor bite

Without mighty effort, and I'd brand hands, and

I filled the trough of water. I press'd the wine.

I fancy'd I'd have a handful of my own,

My own niggers I'd own,

Once Massa free'd me, and got a Big House

Of my own, and catch some persons like dis...

And work with Massa the trade of all men,

The black belt South, planting men, without an end.

Freddy puts the two girls in chains, who are hardly aware, on account of all the alcohol.

FREDDY

Massa is gettin' old now, girls. He needs

Ya' to work hard in dem fields 'fore he gone,

Git on, git on, git, git...

He leads them in circles around the cave, mumbling and humming Spirituals. Stamping his feet to time. He drinks.

FREDDY

I've no man to make more of you, my girls,

That's the managing of more, to man them,

Dat they taught me too, to speak sugars in

Dem dark ears till they'd give it out to him

Or his sons, or some stud field nigger to breed

All the bounty. Git on, git on, git, git...

Git on the guilt, git on, guilt.

Circling circling picking up the swoon and fall, driving, striking.

FREDDY

Uncle SAHM! Here I am as you a man!

I'll own a man to make me a made man,

I'll make a man for SAHM mechanical,

Man the mechanism of the Man mechanical!

All dis' Amerika's machine named SAHM,

Who's draped in the veils of Andrew, a

Mystery more malevolent than any

That's come before, a devil crouching in

The door, way of the South, waying its way

West, all the land to bless,

Will the Whites, damn the rest,

You yourself I'll now show, in the crooked

Mirror of Ferdinando!

They lie down together.

In the morning, five slaves are pulled to the Amerikan cotton.
Freddy's in the field. Freddy, everywhere, a rich black soil,
turning white in curling bulbs, buddings of the cotton branch.

ANDREW JACKSON'S CAMPAIGN
TRAIL – MONTAGE

Now Andrew is running the race. From the stands:

MUCKRAKERS

Rachel Jackson is an incestuous hussy!

A swart lady of the dark, the descendant

Of slave trading miscegenation! [1]

---

[1] rumors are circulated about his wife

CAMPAIGNERS

The efficacy of our elections must not be

Questioned! It's clear that the

General has won![1] Querulous Quincy's

A false President! Make the elevation

Of election a high fair again, vote for

Andrew Jackson!

THE OPPONENT

Demagogue! Caesar! Napoleon! Jackson!

What is the difference between? Accents![2]

ANDREW JACKSON[3]

I am at ease, at peace, regardless of

How the people decide. It is by the

People alone, by their virtue and their

Independence, can make our Republic

A perpetual nation. I will never

Seek nor decline public invitations to Office.

The two gods, Thomas Jefferson, John Adams, die on the
fiftieth Fourth of July. Rockets glare! Bombs burst!

ANDREW JACKSON[4]

I am mate to these men. The Founders father me!

---

[1] he believed the election was stolen from him
[2] he was accused of being a Strong Man
[3] he published the private parts of his letters
[4] he attaches himself to the founding Ancestors

I just as much a father foundering,

Elect me above all US,

I am of you, a People.

THE HERMITAGE – THE SALE OF
BARUNI, DECEMBER 1828

*Now Lyncoya had died from tuberculosis, so Andrew had no
other heirs. But Baruni gave birth to Ammon; she'd heard
him crying since the day he was born. And Andrew began to
raise him. Ammon worked in the big house beside Baruni.*

*Rachel, her eyes looked down on Baruni, a fire in the eyes.
She sells her. Andrew grieves and offers her to a good
master, near the North's belt. Baruni is collar'd, manacle'd,
stood far apart from Ammon, as it were, a gunshot away.*

AMMON
(in arms of Andrew; wailing)

Mama! Mama! Mama!

SLAVE TRADER
(to Baruni)

I'll permit you to tender a kind word…

*Baruni, her eyes glare on Andrew – a blistering gaze – turns
away, let's herself be led.*

RACHEL JACKSON
(scoffing; rubbing her belly)

A mother should weep at such departures...

Ammon strikes Andrew on his scar; he runs to his mother.

AMMON

No! Don't go! No!

BARUNI
(her resolve dissolves)

Oh, my baby! A lash!

What a lash is my love! My son! Ammon!

Andrew! You wicked man! You said you'd nev'r

Separate a mother from her son! Sell

Us both, Andrew, else see hearts cut in two!

Or sell my heart down the river! Buy me

A heart of stone, Andrew! I cannot bear

To feel this wickedness, cruelest commerce!

SLAVE TRADER

That's enough now, mother. The boy'll be fine.

Now you go back up to your Master, boy.

BARUNI
(whispering to Ammon)

What a father you have in Sam, Ammon.

Remember him to reform him.

And make him take your stand.

(shouting to Rachel)

What a father he has for a master!

Remember! Mine came before yours, woman!

Rachel, as if struck, stumbles and swoons into the house.

ANDREW JACKSON

Take her away now! Ammon, to me, now!

Baruni is carried away to a rice plantation. Rachel is laid up in the bed. Three weeks of misery pass for both. Baruni to labor the earth, Rachel at a labor she did not mean.

For Rahcel, look, her belly is swelling out her breasts filling up. She does not bleed in the months. She endures a sharp repetitive or dull pain in the shoulder she does not complain. She sets aside a room for the heir she means to bring out.

She says, I've banished black Baruni, so Sam's conceived a son for me.

While this is conceived, Andrew Jackson is elected the 7th President of Amerika.

THE DEATH OF RACHEL – DECEMBER 22

Andrew and Rachel together in their parlor reading. Andrew reads his wife's face, her belly, her breasts, well of life. Rachel winces. Sharp in the shoulder. She falls out of the chair Andrew holds her carries her to their bed lays her up there three days.

He does not leave her body. She cannot be buried he holds her. His red hair goes grey and white, his face pale and white. Some men separate him, from her, bury her, in the garden in the corner that receives the light rain. He stands over the plot with his cane.

Andrew Jackson does not speak.

No child in Rachel. Andrew Jackson roams the nights and the corridors of the empty Hermitage.

At midmost midnight, SAHM in the rocking chair, rocks it all back and forth, singing quietly to himself. Andrew stands above him, his eyes fallen down, saying nothing.

SAHM

The time is always ready to give birth,
What father would gift, instead of an heir,
A stone, a tomb, a plot of the red earth?
Andrew was old, rounded with age, that's fair,
And Rachel bore more pains from life than labor,
So who could see a son rise from Andrew?
Yet we'd cut covenant, for them my favor,
Yet from her, only wisdom, no sons drew.

Old age should repose on reminiscence,

But fatherless men for sons differed do seek,

To frame themselves farther, in any eyes,

But in glass of black a mirror's too bleak,

Shall he raise that Ammon, a half-black babe?

Or go to Washington?

**WASHINGTON DC –
INAUGURATION DAY, MARCH 4TH,
1829**

*A great crowd come to D.C. to see Andrew Jackson our
President. They watch, of all types all ranks hush as Andrew
mounts the stairs, swears oaths, kisses the book, turns to us,
bows, raises his hands, speaks:*

OUR 7TH PRESIDENT

I a citizen to administer the

Executives of Amerika am.

And as my countrymen clothe me in their

Uniform trust, whose scarlet sacrifices

Stain my blues and whites with patriot's mark,

So I do accept thy animation.

I wear as badge of honor thy honorable mark,

The will of the People, the will of the People,

It is you that makes me. You.

You are Union, en-twin'd in affection

Of sacred Constitution's constant hand,

Your heart shall beat its blood to all corners

Of the continent, from Texas, to the

Edges of Californian oceans, and

Bridges beyond, those endless shining seas,

No boundary shall be for Man such as we,

More freedom, more power impress upon,

Press upon us all to rise, destiny

Manifest in all us men of strong Sam,

You sons of Sam,

Rise, re-stitch thy limbs with his strength, his call,

You inestimable estimators,

You inimitable models of Liberty

Your perseverance swerve!

To the Indians sitting in darkness,

We call you, come out! And live in the West!

A land we will show you, a name we'll name!

Descendants from you, Indians: Amerikans!

Unity, one Amerikan religion…

Forgive me, I'm overcome, the burden,

Of the mountain of Vision is on me,

The North in an unrestrained intercourse

With the South in the same intercourse

With the North and the East in intercourse

With the endless West, all in states combine,
To their descendants descend from me, now
Now, I see my sons are as endless
As the spangled stars of widest heaven,
Whose lights no darknesses of
Division nor foreign power could ever
Darken...
Stars shine in the bluest deep... without end...
One Body lives over US all. Amen.

*The People wave to him swelling up crashing down, on,
around, above, the stairs, swarming swamping suffocating
the President who flees through the midst a parting of them
into a carriage down the road to the White House and within.
They follow in.*

*King Mob. Men, gentlemen, boys, girls, women, slaves,
Blacks, Indians, Irish, in wagons, on carts, off horses, all go
into the White House and stomp about and shout and loot and
lean and leer. Andrew Jackson locks himself in his Cabinet.
Cut glass. Broken China. Sex.*

*Women passed out on the floor. Men fight, bloodying the
floor. His guard sets spiked liquor out on the lawn the People
they spill out the doors and windows to drink. They doze
there. On the White House lawn.*

They sleep, and the doors to the White House are sealed shut.

THE WHITE HOUSE – MIDNIGHT

He wanders the halls, the wide White corridors. His hair is grey, a grey shock. His eyes hang heavy. He cannot sleep.

THE WHITE HOUSE – MIDNIGHT

He wanders the halls, the wide White corridors. His hair is grey, a grey shock. His eyes hang heavy. He cannot sleep.

THE THIRD DREAM OF ANDREW JACKSON – MIDNIGHT

He wanders the wide White corridors.

Andrew, SAHM, into the Oval Office. Rachel there, spread out on the desk, gives birth, boy coming out of what came into her, cut in Andrew's arms, SAHM prompts a name.

            SAHM

Abraham.

            ANDREW

      You will be named Abraham.

            SAHM

Take him by the hand, walk him round the room.

Abraham, in Andrew's hand, reading, listening, fighting, giving, growing, a deep well, filling with rain.

SAHM

Andrew will hear these things.

Put him on the desk. Offer him to me.

Abraham spread on the desk. Look, a knife glitters from Andrew.

ABRAHAM

Where is the lamb?

ANDREW

Sam is himself a lamb.

SAHM

No, I'm not; I will not do that.

ANDREW

Yes, you are; you will so do that.

SAHM

Tie him with ropes, knot him, caught to the desk.

He does as he said.

Shock.

ANDREW

No you will be the lamb, Sam, take his place.

SAHM

No.

ANDREW

Yes.

SAHM

I won't.

ANDREW

I will you, take his place.

SAHM

Light the lamp in your hand, cut a covenant.

He does as he said.

SAHM

Raise the knife.

He does as he said.

SAHM

Cut, covenant.

ANDREW

SAHM's the lamb...

Abraham, in the theatre of the room.

THE WHITE HOUSE – MIDDAY

A lovesick Sam Houston from the far West returns, goes up
to the White House, on Andrew's summons, into the Oval

Office, kneels before a deep red curtain, waits. The curtain parts:[1]

Andrew Jackson throned on a high chair. He has no teeth. He is covered in colored blankets. He stretches forth his hand, wags it over Sam.

ANDREW JACKSON
(laughing)

Tell, how many times did you cane him, Sam?

SAM HOUSTON

Nine times, General, I caned the petty scamp.

ANDREW JACKSON

With a hickory cane?

SAM HOUSTON

           It's of that tree,

Yes, my cane is. He bleated like a lamb,

General, like a pleading poor lamb, dear sir,

It was a humiliation to him.

ANDREW JACKSON

Hahahaha! I'd pay a mighty fee

To see that, Will Stanberry under the lash!

Good Sam! What a return you've made to my

Politics, the punishing of a rival,

---

[1] they recount together: rivalry, war with the federal bank, assassination attempts. They look to a country to come.

As in the days of old! Good on you, Sam!

SAM HOUSTON

They do mean to bring me to trial, sir…

ANDREW JACKSON
(gripping the blankets)

Yes, yes. These thieves, these infernal bank thieves,

They wish to injure your old commander.

SAM HOUSTON

I won't let them, General! I'll contempt the court

If I must – would that relieve you, General!

ANDREW JACKSON

Settle down Sam. Sit down. Listen to me.

I will clothe you, a new suit for you, Sam!

I will go before you, defend you there,

This trial against you, I firmly believe,

Is the greatest act of tyranny and

Usurption' ever attempted under

Our honorable government, but they that

Soil her name shall feel the power of the People-

He doubles over coughing quaking. A slave brings another blanket, wraps it around his thin pale neck. He recovers himself.

ANDREW JACKSON

There's much for the country to accomplish,

171

My cabinet's cleansed, so we've room to roam,

I'll take the axe to the wicked college

Of electorates next, yes, by'eternal,

Sacred elections remain chaste to me,

No Biddle's nor Banks bar me from the People,

Oh it's the People I love, Sam, and they love me,

Oh expanding People, I give you room,

To roam, even to the sun-chasing West,

And your neighbors savage I remove'd

For thy growing pains to gain you legroom,

Running room, and with this you ran me 'gain,

Andrew Jackson, Andrew Jackson I am,

A President re-elected to power,

This or else I naught, a nothing Andrew…

SAM HOUSTON

Forgive me, that I dare speak to you, sir,

I heard there was an attempt on your life…?

ANDREW JACKSON

Richard the third from the push of pages!

Oh mad man of letters! What a word will

Make of a man, beware ye, ye sowers!

For the word becomes a man in adam,

Thorny soil grows a thorny, stinging man.

Yes, Sam, that Richard Lawrence did face me

On the porch of the Capitol, as though

To duel me under the Sovereign's eyes,

In sight of all the People, he raised pistols,

First the one, fired, sparked, fizzled,

Then the second, sparked, fired, fizzled –

Misfires both! I took the cane to him,

The wicked agent of the bank.

SAM HOUSTON

By the eternal, General, this man was an assassin!?

ANDREW JACKSON

He was so, sir! Of course, in court, alibis

Like the asps did hiss – he claimed to be the

Descendant of that wondrous tyrant who

I'd not name again, for fear of his Penman,

The man claimed to be owed an immense

English estate, and that I'd ruined him,

His trade, for he was a mechanical,

With wars against Biddle's Bank, he moaned

My death would restore his estates, titles,

And Albion's crown itself to his head.

He'd murdered his sister for suspecting...

Still, I suspect Biddle made his manipulations

Upon the upturned crown of the mad man,

Regardless, he rots in the asylum.

SAM HOUSTON

General, these pistols, they were defective?

ANDREW JACKSON

No sir! By eternity, no! They fired

Fine and true on afterward tests, true shots!

SAM HOUSTON

General, the hand of Sam must be on you,

Such providential protection proves it.

ANDREW JACKSON

P-p-p! Yes I suspect it so, Sam, I suspect.

Now, on to the end I've summoned you to.

Sam, listen to me now.

SAM HOUSTON

I'm here, listening.

ANDREW JACKSON

I am very old, my better blessings,

They're behind me, far away behind me,

I must see straight ahead, see to the next

Of me, walking into the future now,

I see a successor succeeding me,

I hear the trail of footsteps of followers,

Walking over the high hill of the West,

Sam, servant, put your hand under my thigh…

He does as he said.

174

ANDREW JACKSON

Sam, his eyes shall be deep red with a wine,

He shall go to my home, the West, to find

A wife for my endless sons, bringing her

Out for them, Sam will be with you, Sam… go!

He does as he said.

Sam leaves for Texas, millions in his hands. Andrew draws back behind the deep red curtain. He waits there, cold, and covered in black blankets.

ACT V

Texas. Now, in that land, there was much discontent among the Amerikans. They had outgrown their boundaries. They grew up into Texas, expanding, living everywhere there. The Mexicans are afraid of this immigration, the importation of slavery, the elimination of Nativity. They want them out.

THE WELL OF TEXAS – 1836

Weary from the way, the desert, the sun, Sam Houston stakes his tent by a well. He waits for water to come to him. Women are coming out to him with water the way war brings blood. He selects one.

The girl of an indiscernible ancestry. Brown skin, arctic eyes. Her hair jet. She carried the jug to the well, lowering, filling with cool clear cold.

SAM HOUSTON

Girl! Girl! Bring me some water, will you not?

She does as he says.

SAM HOUSTON

Sit here a moment, girl. Please, what's your name?

THE GIRL

You're an Amerikan?

177

SAM HOUSTON

I am, yes mam.

THE GIRL

There're lot of Amerikans in Texas.

SAM HOUSTON

You are from Texas? You are a squaw, mam?

THE GIRL

I'm from South Carolina. Ancestry,

That I do not know; I may be Indian,

White, Negro, Spanish, Maya, there are too

Many accounts of ancestors of me

To say it's that one: This is me.

SAM HOUSTON

Thank you

For the water, I've traveled many miles

Through the desert. Look, here is a scroll that

I hold – it bears the seal of the President –

I am an important servant, with an

Important mission: will you help me, mam?

THE GIRL

As much as I may I'll help you.

SAM HOUSTON

Name's Sam.

Where were you born in South Carolina?

THE GIRL

The Waxhaw's sir, a place of no notables.

SAM HOUSTON

Now you must stay by my side, for my
General is born of the red clay of there,
And he's a most notable man, therefore
You are most noticeable to me, mam.

THE GIRL

As you say, Sam. But tell me, what I can
Do for you.

SAM HOUSTON

War is coming to Texas.

THE GIRL

War is Texas. Here you are not notable,
Here, men of war are like mounds of sand.

SAM HOUSTON

No mam, no mam, I'm sent of a President.

THE GIRL

It's better to drink the cool water from
The well with a woman, than to fare war
In the desert on the whims of a man.

SAM HOUSTON

Even a *Great Man*'s whim?

THE GIRL

The whim's the worse

179

In great man, their ways… is like… ocean-ing

The desert with your handfuls of water.

SAM HOUSTON

Don't you know, mam – there's honor in our war?

THE GIRL

Is there water left in your cup?

SAM HOUSTON

Why, yes…

THE GIRL

Put your finger in the cup.

SAM HOUSTON

Alright. 'Tis.

THE GIRL

Now pull your finger out. See how the water

Returns to its place? The finger is the

Lifespan of the man.

Now water knows his space no more.

Meanwhile…

MEXICO CITY – JANUARY 1833

Now General Santa Ana is marching into Tenochtitlan, the head of many soldiers. All the men women slaves free laborers rich poor natives all follow him into the President's

house engulfing adulating venerating praising powering.
King Mob. Santa Ana. [1]

AT THE WELL OF TEXAS – 1836

SAM HOUSTON

You are wise for your age. But you don't know
My General.

THE GIRL

A General is generic.

SAM HOUSTON

He's led many men to victory he's
Conquered the continent, taken cities
For Sam, for Sam, brought glory to his name,
For Amerika, prestige and power,
For the People, sovereignty and power,
For the common man, suffrage and power.

THE GIRL

A man may make men murder, mar themselves,
Burn homes, butcher brothers, and rape mothers,
And they may cheer for it, and live with it,
But that is no victory to me, no,
No glory's in broken hearts, or breaking

---

[1] look, the war hero of the revolution marches into
the Capitol, declares himself President

181

Of hearts, nor prestige in power's push,

Power pushes that on itself alone,

And your sovereignty's so selective,

Seems more a servitude – when the sovereign

Says so your suffrage seems so – you vote votes,

And a great man goes up the stage, and names

Himself catchingly common, with catch,

For seeming to have representation,

Your power's only, after all, but the

Delusion of family resemblance.

THE CAMP OF THE TEXAS MILITIA
– MIDDAY

A Watchman strange goes into Sam's tent.

SAM HOUSTON

Please speak. What does my General need of me?

THE WATCHMAN

You will instigate the impressions of fear,

Indians on edges, spilling oe'r the brim,

Five thousand Creek invading this Texas,

And the atrocities of Santa Ana,

The raping of the white women, coming

Here forcefully the mustering of men

Amerikan incites the ire of him,

And the man of war will come with his war,

Lead him to the Sabine; we'll meet him there.

SAM HOUSTON

Draw them into an *Amerikan* war...

THE WATCHMAN

Not only Texas, but the stretches of

California too, seas to shining seas,

He will round with waist.

**THE CAMP OF THE TEXAS MILITIA
– EVENING**

*Sam and the Girl of the well wander through the war camp,
camped outside San Antonio and the Alamo. The songs of
fiddlers, singers, cowboys and play and stomping their feet.
She leads him to them.*

THE SINGER

(singing)

'Oh, give me a home where the buffalo roam,

Where the deer and the antelope play;

Where seldom is heard a discouraging word,

And the skies are not cloudy all day.[1]'

THE COWBOYS

(singing)

Home, home on the range,

Where the deer and the antelope play;

---

[1] Anachronistically, they sing a song of a unified Texas

Where seldom is heard a discouraging word
And the skies are not cloudy all day!

THE SINGER
        (singing)

Where the air is so pure, the zephyrs so free,
The breezes so balmy and light,
That I would not exchange my home on the range
For all the cities so bright.

THE COWBOYS
        (singing)

The red man was pressed from this part of the West,
He's likely no more to return
To the banks of Red River where seldom if ever
Their flickering campfires burn.

THE SINGER
        (singing)

How often at night when the heavens are bright
With the light of the glittering stars,
Have I stood here amazed and asked as I gazed
If their glory exceeds that of ours...

He notices the Girl noticing him he stops and looks on her.
She smiles, radiant and bright.

THE SINGER

Well, howdy there, girl.

THE GIRL

> Spin me a yarn, sir?

THE SINGER

Why, I will then.

(lays down his instrument)

In Texas, the air's so pure that people ne'er die,
Excepting by accident. No gents, it was just not
Possible for a Man to die when he was in Texas, all
Purities of the atmosphere and the prairie prevented
It. So when persons got too old to be useful no mo',
They just thinned out and got carried off by a strong
Breeze, clear outta Texas, to die an Amerikan on
Amerikan soil. That's a fact, upon my honor as a
Cowboy. Indeed, I knew a certain philanthropic
Gentleman who built for himself a museum in our
Texas, where Texans who were too old, thin and
Leathery like cowhide, could stay bundled up into
Labeled sacks, registered and hung up. So if their
Friends or family might wish to converse with
Them, swap yarns, or just generally jaw, they'd
Have a known place to find 'em, instead of hunting
Through the air for the stray drifters. For a fine fee
Of fifty cents, an old friend would be taken down,
Placed in a kettle of tepid water, which would soon
Enable him to converse as well as any hustler round

The gambling green. Why, he could hold

A conversation as long as half an hour before

He'd dry and thin out again, then get hung up

Again in his place-

A COWBOY

-Tarnation! That's a tall tale if eva' I heard one!

THE SINGER

It is nevertheless true, young whelp. I know's it true

On account a going to the museum once myself.

I was looking for my ol' uncle, Sammy Hawley.

He'd gone up to the Rocky Mountains some forty

Years before and still hadn't come back down.

The clerk there examined his register, with a

Searchin and stern eye, looking through all the list

Without even a single blink on hundred, nay,

Thousands of pages he gave his gander to, at last,

He found my uncle's name, black'd in that fateful

List. Number 3376, he'd been hung up there some

Twenty two years, clerk said. I paid my fee and

Requested he be brought down from all those miles

Of shelves tall as a mountain. The rude contents of

The sack spilled out into the water like a strip of old

Jerky into a trough, expanded, wetted, grew, till my

Uncle Sammy was before me as young lookin as

The day I said, 'Well, bye'. He seemed pleased

To see me, though I was young as a sapling when

He last eye'd me, and bout as short as a sapling then

Too. He asked after my father, my mother, some

Old friends. I told him, with as much tact as I could

Muster, that, sadly, they'd all died in the long days

Between now and then. His voice was very weak…

Could only talk for bout, maybe, twenty minutes I'd

Reckon, when he hissed that the breath was failing

Him, and he was drying out too much again, like

The desert in the morning… Excepting I had

Something else to say, he'd like to be hung up again

On all dem shelves. I remarked, asking after a fine

Gun I knew he once owned. He said he'd done hid

It up on the crossbeam of his rafters of his cabin

He'd situated on the peak of the Divide, and that

I was welcome to take the legendary arms up,

Should I will it so. I thanked him and bid him,

'Well, bye'. Then he was light and thin and leathery

Nough to pick him up between two fingers, which

The clerk then did, then vanished down the dark

Maze of shelves, taking'm to his particular locality

In eternity. I still got his gun, I done hiked all the

Way up there. I've never fired it, no, boys I reckon I

Never will. If you ever stumble on that old

Museum, boys, be sure to pay a visit to the old

Timers there, for they like a good talk in all that

Quiet.

The crackling of the campfire; the digestion of the meal in the gut; the cackling of the cowboys their cares caught for a moment. The Girl, she thanks the singer, gives him a cup of water, goes among the camp, giving the water to the whole camp, from her well pitcher. Sam follows her into the night.

REBECCA

What is the end of war? No end. No end.

SAN ANTONIO – BLOOD DAWN

In the morning the Texans cross the cottonwood trees and encroach upon San Antonio and storm the fortress called Alamo and they lose seven men in the skirmish of that movement, but they take the fortress and sequester themselves within and wait for General Santa Ana and his unprepared men and uninspired conscripts and un-communicable Indians to approach them.

THE ALAMO AND GOLIAD –
MARCH 6TH 1836 - MARCH 27TH 1836

Look, there is no mercy for them. On the thirteenth day the degüello played in the pipes and brass and drum of the Mexican bands their bugles call'd for the beheading of Texans. Instrument, canon. Boom. Boom. Boom. They come up over the walls on ladders; they flow through the burst and crumbled walls like water through a dam. The Texan cannons thin their ranks, but they fill their broken ranks like water returning to its place. ¡No rendirse, muchachos! Give them hell! Remember!

To the barracks...To the chapel of white stones... To the windows carved in the walls...

The kicking against the pricks, the springing from the corral, the galloping of desperate men across the prairie out... the catching of them under the sharp saber and the pinto's mottled hoof.

Davy Crockett standing tall on the low wall of the white church he wields his gun as a club, as his flag, as an Amerikan full-bloodied and bloodying – his arms swing!

The cannon knocking down the door. The volley of fire. The fighting of hands on hands in there in all the doors all the men ensconced therein their lights go out in blazes. James

Bowie bedridden his head raised with much effort his pistols raised with more effort his knife in his left hand his Bowie knife falling from there and the bayonet's good riddance.

The last Amerikan men, they go into the church and kneel in it with the light in the chapel the sparkling light of the canon's fuse the canon firing its tremendous shock in the chapel's sacre, like thunders of the god, the bolts of Texas, out the double doors, into men, and then the flood coming in.

The Mexicans, look, they bayonet the bodies that move they shoot the bodies that are still they fire on themselves in the confusion of the rushing desire.

Seven Amerikan men are lined up against the white wall. Davy Crocket there. The begging in the mouths for life the panting of the exertion of death the last words are prayers or whimpers put on parched lips or:

DAVY CROCKETT
I am rejoiced at my fate.
SANTA ANNA
No mercy.

Look, Texans become their State, in the air, moving with the wind, moving everywhere.

And at Goliad no more mercy from these goliath's shall the Amerikans receive on the 27th of March, a Sunday. The four hundred and twelve young men, Texans, race of rangers, matchless in yarn and song, brave, boys all, will be marched down the road under the Palms between the two rows of Mexicans just as much boys, just as much matchless, just as much under the Sword, but one must murder the other, both will be debased, but one must be shot down close enough to shake hands, both must be knifed and clubbed and clutch in the dirt for mothers and those that could not walk they will be smothered in their beds and their captain, Fannin, shall see this and be tortured and the seeing of this were also the tortures and he will ask for his belongings to be given to family members and to be shot in the heart and for his body to be buried in Texas, and he asks for the same mercies for his boys, whom he loves now more than ever, at the ending.

Fannin will be robbed, shot in the face, his body burned his boys burned in a pile of boys.

Black smoke on a noon day in Texas. The sun is bloody through it.

SANTA ANA
(atop his black horse)

Fuego elegante, un asunto tan elegante...

THE MARCH OF THE ARMY OF
TEXAS TO THE SABINE –
AFTERNOON

Rebecca of the well, she is waiting for you, Sam, up the column of soldiers, up the line of women.

He goes to her, walks beside her for a while, watches her, listens to her talk.

REBECCA
(to the non-combatants)

Take and drink. For a wife to weep is well,

To make the marks of sorrow on the cheek

Is the sign and show of a careful grief,

But the desert is a long way, a walk

Not untaken unwisely, take and drink,

My Water is health to you, will allow

That wailing and that howling for husbands

Whom you have lost, or whom you are losing,

Or will lose in the eroding of time,

My desert will know your grief, a desert

Will be a sea once again, for your salt

And your water will care to carve these stones,

These great rocks, spires, red rocks that watch hills,

These mesas like the meal tables of gods,

Of ancient men and of ancient women,

Giant forms, of the old tales told through time,

These vales with lines of time in sediment,

Sediment, sediments enstacked on each,

And these hillocks and tabletops, reveal

The remains of me, unveil me, Atlantic,

You, women, will carve this bed as the sea did,

Your tears will shape and mold this just as much,

Your howls' wind shall erode thus just as much,

Just as much as the sea

You moan for your castaways,

You beat the shores with your fists,

You cover, and you uncover,

Take and drink and weep and howl and wail

And will, will the desert to a garden

A gain, the desert will grow green,

Again, seas will recede, and reveal Me serene.

He fills his cup from her ladle. He takes her aside the column.

SAM HOUSTON

Whose daughter are you?

REBECCA

I was born to a mother, Bethel,

She was a woman of many races,

But the fathering one, as she told me,

Was a Scottish man, and an immigrant,

193

Of Ulster there, but an Amerikan

When he went to her, so when I came out

I was Amerikan, born on the 4th,

The country being only twenty-five years

In the youth of its life.

SAM HOUSTON

My General is also of that family.

He does not often talk of his boyhood,

But much of what I've learned from many years

Of service I've stored up in this my mind,

And knowing him well, I know he's a man

Of a great heart, I know he'd yearn to hear

That a trace of family remains to him.

Rebecca, go to Andrew with me…

He's a man that burns for a family.

REBECCA

(hurrying away)

A woman with child needs me, excuse me, Sam.

SAM HOUSTON

Rebecca! Rebecca!

REBECCA

Another time we'll talk, dear sir! Goodbye!

BEFORE THE BATTLE, THE SABINE RIVER – NIGHT

Now the Amerikan army, sent by the 7ᵗʰ President, was waiting on the other side of the river for Santa Ana to cross, and it was Sam's order to lead Santa Ana over that river.

Sam Houston had gained many men after the massacres, many joining the militia. The Texans are itching for a fight, they'll not flee any further, despite Sam's orders they dig in, ready themselves. Sam's sleepless among the tents.

He looks for Rebecca, does not find her. He finds Santa Ana, his army arriving, waiting for him & the red morning.

THE BATTLE OF SAN JACINTO – MORNING

The battle was won for Texas in the morning. Santa Ana was fleeing through the bayou, hid in a soldier's common shirt. Texans bind him, bring him into the camp, the Mexicans salute, stand at attention for him; so Santa Ana was found.

They bring him to Sam. Sam Houston reclines under a mossy oak. He fiddles with a sprig thrust into moss. His foot's shot. His foot was wound in wraps. Santa Ana stands there.

THE TEXANS

Kill him, Sam! Remember Goliad!

Remember the Alamo! No mercy, Sam!
SAM HOUSTON

Sir, what say you in your defense?
SANTA ANA
(as translated from the Spanish)

I will order my army to retreat, back to Mexico, and

The territories for which you've fought I'll cede to

You forever. Amerika will grow to the Rio Grande.
THE TEXANS

Mexican lies. He's promising what we're

Already taking. We say put him down.
SAM HOUSTON

I reckon I should not show you mercy,

For you gave none to mine.

Enter, Watchman, whispers in Sam's ear.

SAM HOUSTON

Santa Ana, you're going to Washington.

Adjunct, bind him and bow him, he's a gift

For General Jackson. See that the prisoners

Here are treated well, for we're not like him.

I will send dispatches to Urrea,

And see that the Mexicans cross over, and

That they leave our slaves behind for us to collect.

THE ADJUNCT

Yes, Sam! Hurrahs for Sam! Raise a high shout!

The Texans' whoop goes high up. Santa Ana's bound, led out.

THE TEXAN CAMP – EVENING

Sam found Rebecca in a burial tent by a dead man on the bier. She's wound him in bandages, cleaning his face, hiding the wounds. She buttons his shirt, ties his shoes. Sets his hat on straight and low over the brow.

SAM HOUSTON
(sitting beside her)

Here mam, allow me to help with that please.

This was'a brave boy you prepare for his grave.

REBECCA

He is still brave.

SAM HOUSTON
(nodding)

I suspect that is so.

REBECCA

You know his name?

SAM HOUSTON

Yes… Robert was his name,

Is, pardon me mam. He is, I recall,

An immigrant, slipped over the border

Into Texas with his folks, like many of

These young boys, he'd known no other

Land than the one he grew up in: Texas.

                    REBECCA

His family survives him?

                    SAM HOUSTON

                              I am drafting

A letter to them, so I suspect so, yes.

Family... Family is a precious thing, mam.

Don't you think it so, mam?

                    REBECCA

                              Who's your family?

                    SAM HOUSTON

Mine? Why, I had none for much time, grew up

With the Cherokees in Tennessee, under

The name Raven, just as free as that bird

I was then, all skies and forest my home,

And an Indian chief for a father

Named John Jolly, with whom I needed not

Suffer jargons of hellfire and damnation,

But I drank from the wells of deep water,

Of the Great Spirit,

And how She filled every mountain and blade

Of the endless land, that my educating,

That with the words of the great Greek Poet,

I needed nothing else, became a man

Before I could grow a beard, I reckon.

When the Britannic giant came stomping

Down on the country, I joined the nearest

Militia, met General Jackson, never

Looked on another man as a father

Other than him, so grand he is to me.

REBECCA

Do you have any children?

SAM HOUSTON

No.

REBECCA

You do.

SAM HOUSTON

How's that?

REBECCA

Man with no children... fathers on

Whatever he can father on.

SAM HOUSTON

That so?

REBECCA

Men scarce know what a fatherhood is,

They fear what their deeds with women produce,

But on every woman, man, child, land, thing,

199

Their imagination's seeds'r profuse,

Men'll make all the world their sons if they could

Sow it so, and the less sons a man has father'd

The fiercer the urge to found what he may,

What a man's feared he's fled to all along,

And if he'll not enter the woman the

Woman will her aspects turn to what pleases

Him more, attracting, grafting him without

Regard to his protests machismo,

So a woman makes the world without end,

Mending man to her ends.

SAM HOUSTON

You're a mighty strong woman, mam…

REBECCA

You're too much a Sam for me, sir…

SAM HOUSTON

You mistake me mam, I mean that your strength

Does recall to me another's, and nudges

A notion of family resemblance that's

Mighty strong, mam; it's mighty strong, mam.

REBECCA

(angry)

I'm not related to him, sir!

SAM HOUSTON

Why'd you

Say so!? He's a grand man, the grandest there is!

REBECCA

(pausing)

Men have moved grand things, and mastered

Themselves, masters over each other, moved

Mountains, made war, won war, made wives

Of the wars, but this does not make them grand.

SAM HOUSTON

Than what makes men grand, mam?

REBECCA

Their fatherhood.

SAM HOUSTON

My General's the father of a Nation.

REBECCA

That's a false fatherhood.

Her brother enters the tent, a man of mixed ancestry. He
bows his head to Sam, looks to Rebecca, says:

THE BROTHER

Bought time to head out now it is, Becca'.

Begging your pardon, General sir.

SAM HOUSTON

Who's this?

REBECCA

My brother. It's time we moved on now, sir.

SAM HOUSTON

Where will you go?

THE BROTHER

Spirit moves with the wind.

SAM HOUSTON

Flowing, rolling, moving, everywhere...

This my last plea, Sam has blessed my General,

Many gifts he would give to you, mother

To a nation you'd be...

REBECCA

(leaving the tent)

May *you* be a father of thousands, sir.

Look, Sam Houston becomes the first President of the Republic of Texas. A city there is named after him to this very day.

THE WHITE HOUSE – NIGHT

A Watchman led Santa Ana by the hand up to the bedroom. President Andrew Jackson sits on the bed, beside a single lamp, in his nightshirt, showing his bullet marks, his gaunt frame pale skin scar on the forehead sunk in the skull, the parasites living in the man, whose white hair's thick and wild, ejecting from and projecting his head.

ANDREW JACKSON

Sit down, General.

He does as he said.

ANDREW JACKSON

How much power hold you over Mexico?

SANTA ANA

I am still a god.

ANDREW JACKSON

And your promises are as true as one?

SANTA ANA

Claro[1]. Yes.

ANDREW JACKSON

They've deposed you in your absence.

SANTA ANA

They love me, they fear me. One tops… other,

Then the other tops it. Santa Ana

Is still Señor of the… amarío[2].

ANDREW JACKSON

And if I shall spirit you away to

Veracruz, that mound you could again climb?

SANTA ANA

Sí sí sí! Yes, President, I am Santa Ana.

Santa Ana. I am master all men.

---

[1] clearly
[2] wardrobe

ANDREW JACKSON

(chuckling; coughing; rattling)

Clearly… clearly… clearly you are, General.

But for your return there are terms, *my* terms.

Santa Ana leans back in the chair grins his wide white teeth and nods.

ANDREW

You, sir, will formally sell to me the

Territories, Texas and California,

For the fairest price of three and a half

Million Amerikan dollars in gold.

Santa Ana there, grinning.

SANTA ANA

Dalo por hecho. No te puedo decir que no[1].

I say, *yes*, President, *yes, yes* to you.

ANDREW JACKSON

Then you'll see Veracruz soon, young man.

Andrew Jackson will hold you to your word.

Now Amerikans don't take kindly to

Broken treaties, and when we want something,

We don't let it taken out our teeth.

---

[1] take it for granted. I can't tell you no.

SANTA ANA

How many teeth do you have left, President?

ANDREW

(grins: mostly grey gums)

Enough to flow your throat, by eternal.

SANTA ANA

Hahahaha…

ANDREW JACKSON

Hahahaha… Watchman!

The Watchman enters the bedroom.

ANDREW JACKSON

See this wee man to his boat; he's a long

Way to go yet. Git on.

Santa Ana stands, bows deeply, lets himself be led out.

Andrew Jackson, scars in his lungs, coughs & rattles all night

long. He does not sleep. He wanders the wide white halls.

AN ORPHAN ASYLUM,
WASHINGTON D.C.
– CHRISTMAS EVE MORNING

Now Andrew Jackson was very fond of all the orphans of the

city. He funded much of their needs. And one Christmas Eve

morning, he left his White House early to visit them.

He burst through the door with gifts! He's swarmed with children. He gives to each: drums, wind up soldiers, china dolls with rope hair, bridles and saddles and wooden guns, tea sets, rattles, sparklers, hoops and sticks, carrots, puddings, and other spoils.

AN ORPHAN BOY

Nuncle! Nuncle! Listen to me a moment!

ANDREW

(sitting him on his knee)

What is it, dear boy? Andrew's here, listenin'.

AN ORPHAN BOY

Nuncle, oh you'd never lie to me,

I know, have you ever seen Santa Claus?

Hush in the room, all the children, listening to the tallest thinnest oldest man they'd ever seen.

ANDREW

No, no, my dear boy, Andrew's not seen him.

AN ORPHAN BOY

Emily thinks he may not come tonight.

Did you ever know him to behave so?

ANDREW

Well my children, we can only wait and see,

And if Santa didn't come, I think it the

Duty of every little boy and girl

To be cheerful none the less, for that's Christmas,

You see, to smile bright on your neighbor that

Holy light that shines and lives on all smiles.

Children, Andrew once knew a little boy,

As young as you, who not only never

Heard of Christmas or Santa Claus, but ne'er

Held a toy in his life, and after the

Death of his mother, a purest, saintly

Woman, a saint even more than she was

Woman, the boy had neither home nor friends,

The boy had nobody at all... not e'en

An old Andrew to drop in every

Once in a while, bestowing love and toys.

ALL THE CHILDREN

Poor little fellow! Had he lived with us,

We would have shared all our playthings with him!

ANDREW

Yes, my children, I suspect you would have.

AN ORPHAN BOY

Nuncle, Nuncle, what happened to the boy?

ANDREW

(gathering them to him)

He *took* the gift he'd wanted be given.

207

Black slaves bring in snowballs of starch-coated cotton. They play around the orphan room, Andrew, and the other orphans.

THE HERMITAGE, TENNESSEE
– 1845

Out of office, Andrew kneels before Rachel's grave.

ANDREW

(to the grave)

Dear heart, daily I bring water to thy

Cold earthen bed, with my tears be-dew

The blankets of morning soil, with voice thy form

Beneath I warm. If my voice's too cold

By chills of age, then I'll lay this thin

Rail of a ragged body on the place

And pray to push what life's left in me out,

Under the mound, into the box, unto

The preserved lips a breath longing enough

To wake you.

If this too I cannot do, then I'll await the change:

Of Resurrection

To Rachel, body awefully in union,

Reunion joyfully bound,

Unite our states, in crush of buried dust.

THE DEATH OF ANDREW JACKSON
– SUNDAY, JUNE 8TH 1845, 6 PM

Daily he takes the medicines of alcohol, opium, and cocaine.
He lies in the bed, all the wards and slaves and friends of his
estate around him. He has gone blind. His eyes' white like
the white of the shock of hair that hangs amazingly over his
throning brow, like a living creature. Fever. Scarlet auge.
His skin holds him in place. His final will:

ANDREW JACKSON

Will H. Harrison will be struck down by Sam,

For he's shown his contempt for him throughout

The land – his failure to acquire Texas

And California – Sam shall not stand

For weak men in his White House, so it's so.

James Polk will make the marriage of US,

The Husband shall meet his Bride of the West,

Unspotted bride, white foam, on the shores of

The Pacific sea, all the Gold in-b'tween,

Where is Sam Houston?

A VOICE

He's on his way, father.

ANDREW JACKSON

I demand him arrive! I demand... I demand him!

Sam... Sam...

(delirium)

In all! The creation of Amerika,

Also its fall!

A divorce in the marriage of the West...

Two brothers, in one womb, struggling there,

For the first to fall into the wide Womb,

One brother, red, one brother, moon, but my

Sons both, one usurping the other, one

Usurping the other, heel-clutchers both.

A VOICE

Go to the earth again, father.

ANDREW
(choking)

I will!

Not while I will!

A VOICE

Go to the earth again, father.

ANDREW
(hallucinating)

I see!

I see the god! George Washington! He is

In my midst with the keys of eight heavens!

He says, all go to the Amerikan heaven!

White and black both, and men and women both!

He leads me up to the gates, I see SAHM,

All along, SAHM, in the

Amerikan heaven a name's a-writ,

Says SAHM is in me, and I am in he,

And we are one in the imagining

Of *this* that is, our Amerikan country,

Hear me… hear me…

A VOICE

Go to the earth, father.

ANDREW

Where is my son? Where is my boy?

A VOICE

Your sons as numerous as the spangled stars…

ANDREW

But none can hold my hand,

This hand, this instrument of SAHM… Is the

Country a consolation for the pale hand

That quivers and shakes, on the edge of the

Deathbed? What was my music? All of it

Was good was that which made the moment great,

I count and note as notes each particular

Scar, wound, and gash, know the groans that war

Instrument'ed on me here, there, a song

Everywhere, a sound symphony,

A skin's a sheet of music, played poverty,

Played majesty and messiah!

Played by me played by he,

Songs of endless, rounding eternity,

Mother, the last palm you placed on my cheek…

Brother… bumps I read on cheek, an augury…

I am content with this piece, this sound,

And the rest of the song I read is peace,

That an Andrew nothing, I again am.

Eternity is writ on Vanity.

A VOICE

All the Amerikans are here to see you off.

ANDREW

So I am in you, so you are in me.

A VOICE

Go to the earth, father. SAHM has much more
Fathers to find than you.

*Look, he does as they said. The thin pale hand quivers,
grasps, yearns no longer. And an Andrew Jackson is dead.*

*Sam Houston arrives, brings his boy to the head of the bed,
holding him to him, saying to both:*

SAM HOUSTON
(*weeping*)

My son, try to remember that you have

Looked on the face of one Andrew Jackson.

THE FUNERAL OF ANDREW
JACKSON – MORNING

The parrot was cursing his favorite words. The congregation

was singing her favorite song:

THE SINGERS
(singing 'How firm a foundation, ye
saints of the Lord', Rachel's song)

'When through the deep waters I call thee to go,

The rivers of sorrow shall not overflow;

For I will be with thee, thy troubles to bless,

And sanctify to thee thy deepest distress.

When through fiery trials thy pathway shall lie,

My grace, all sufficient, shall be thy supply;

The flame shall not hurt thee; I only design

Thy dross to consume, and thy gold to refine.

E'en down to old age all My people shall prove

My sovereign, eternal, unchangeable love;

And then, when grey hairs shall their temples adorn,

Like lambs they shall still in My bosom be borne.'

A MOURNER

Do you think the General will go to heaven?

ALFRED

If d'General wants to go, who's gonna stop him?

They bury him by Rachel in the garden.

213

Andrew Jackson, everywhere, a rich red clay. Everywhere.
His statue is in the streets. His stature stands far above the
streets. His stride is in the skies, his long legs, walking with
the sun, chasing the West the way out West. He is everywhere.
Jackson, Alabama; Jackson, Mississippi; Jackson, Missouri.

SOMEWHERE IN ILLINOIS
– EVENING

Abraham was walking through the pines when he found a
stone well, covering itself with bramble and with brake.
Abraham broke it away. Down its deep he looked:

> SAHM

Hello.

> ABRAHAM

  Hello.

> SAHM
>
> May I come up and out?

EPILOG

An old man, Private John G. Burnett, of Captain Abraham McClellan's Company, 2nd Regiment, 2nd Brigade, Mounted Infantry, in full uniform, wheels into the room of an abandoned Amerikan Museum. Alone. A birthday cake there, on a modest chair, with eighty candles burning bright.

JOHN G. BURNETT[1]

It is my birthday, December the 11th 1890. I am Eighty years old today. I was born at King's Iron Works in Sullivan County, Tennessee, December The 11th, 1810. I grew into manhood fishing in Beaver Creek and roaming through the forest Hunting the Deer, the wild Boar, and the timber Wolf. Often, I spending weeks at a time in the Solitary wilderness, with no companions but my Rifle, hunting knife, and a small hatchet that I Carried in my belt. On these long hunting trips I Met and became acquainted with many of the Cherokee Indians, hunting with them by day and Sleeping around their camp fires by night. I learned To speak their language, and they taught me the arts

[1] His first-hand account has been gathered from a letter to his children, and is cited at the end of this book

Of trailing and building traps and snares. On one of
My long hunts in the fall of 1829, I found a young
Cherokee who had been shot by a roving band of
Hunters, and who had eluded his pursuers and
Concealed himself under a shelving rock. Weak
From loss of blood, the poor creature was unable to
Walk and almost famished for water. I carried him
To a spring, bathed and bandaged the bullet wound,
Built a shelter out of bark peeled from a dead
Chestnut tree, nursed and protected him, feeding
Him on chestnuts and roasted deer meat. When he
Was able to travel, I accompanied him to the home
Of his people and remained so long that I was given
Up for lost. By this time, I had become an expert
Rifleman and fairly good archer and a good trapper
And spent most of my time in the forest in quest of
Game… The removal of the Cherokee Indians from
Their lifelong homes in the year of 1838 found me a
Young man in the prime of life and a Private soldier
In the Amerikan Army. Being acquainted with
Many of the Indians and able to fluently speak their
Language, I was sent as interpreter into the Smoky
Mountain Country in May, 1838, and witnessed the
Execution of the most brutal order in the History of

Amerikan Warfare. I saw the helpless Cherokees
Arrested and dragged from their homes and driven
At the bayonet point into the stockades. And in the
Chill of a drizzling rain on an October morning I
Saw them loaded like cattle or sheep into six
Hundred and forty-five wagons and started toward
The west. One can never forget the sadness and
Solemnity of that morning. Chief John Ross led in
Prayer, and when the bugle sounded and the
Wagons started rolling, many of the children rose to
Their feet and waved their little hands good-by to
Their mountain homes, knowing they were leaving
Them forever. Many of these helpless people did
Not have blankets, and many of them had been
Driven from home barefooted. On the morning of
November the 17th, we encountered terrific sleet,
And snowstorms with freezing temperatures and
From that day until we reached the end of the
Fateful journey on March 26th, 1839, the sufferings
Of the Cherokees were awful. The trail of the exiles
Was a trail of death. They had to sleep in the
Wagons and on the ground without fire. And I have
Known as many as twenty-two of them to die in one
Night of pneumonia due to ill treatment, cold, and

Exposure. Among this number was the beautiful Christian wife of Chief John Ross. This noble Hearted woman died a martyr to childhope, giving Her only blanket for the protection of a sick child. She rode thinly clad through a blinding sleet and Snowstorm, developed pneumonia, and died in the Still hours of a bleak winter night, with her head on Lieutenant Greggs' saddle blanket. I made the long Journey to the west with the Cherokees and did all That a Private soldier could do to alleviate their Sufferings. When on guard duty at night I had Many times walked my beat in my blouse in order That some sick child might have my overcoat.

I was on guard duty the night Mrs. Ross died. When relieved at midnight I did not retire, but Remained around the wagon out of sympathy for Chief Ross, and at daylight was detailed by Captain McClellan to assist in the burial for the other Unfortunates who died on the way. Her uncoffined Body was buried in a shallow grave by the roadside Far from her native mountain home, and the Sorrowing Cavalcade moved on. Being a young Man, I mingled freely with the young women and Girls. I have spent many pleasant hours with them

When I was supposed to be under my blanket, and
They had many times sung their mountain songs to
Me, this being all that they could do to repay my
Kindness. And with all my association with Indian
Girls from October 1829 to March 26th 1839, I did
Not meet one who was a moral prostitute. They are
Kind and tender-hearted and many of them are
Beautiful. The only trouble that I had with anybody
On the entire journey to the west was a brutal
Teamster by the name of Ben McDonal, who was
Using his whip on an old feeble Cherokee to hasten
Him into the wagon. The sight of that old and
Nearly blind creature quivering under the lashes of
A bull whip was too much for me. I attempted to
Stop McDonal, it ended in a personal encounter.
He lashed me across the face, the wire tip on his
Whip cutting a bad gash in my cheek. The little
Hatchet that I carried in my hunting days was in my
Belt… so McDonal was carried unconscious from
The scene. I was placed under guard, but Ensign
Henry Bullock and Private Elkanah Millard had
Both witnessed the encounter. They gave Captain
McClellan the facts; I was never brought to trial.
The long painful journey to the West ended March

26th, 1839, with four thousand silent graves
Reaching from the foothills of the Smoky
Mountains to what is known as Indian territory in
The West. And covetousness on the part of the
White race was the cause of all that the Cherokees
Had to suffer. Ever since Ferdinand De Soto made
His journey through the Indian country in the year
Of 1540, there had been a tradition of a rich Gold
Mine somewhere in the Smoky Mountain Country,
And I think the tradition was true. At a festival at
Echata on Christmas night 1829, I danced
With Indian girls who were wearing ornaments
Around their necks that looked like Gold.
In the year of 1829, a little Indian boy living on
Ward creek had sold a Gold nugget to a White
Trader, and that nugget sealed the doom of the
Cherokees. In a short time, the country was
Overrun with armed brigands claiming to be
Government Agents, who paid no attention
To the rights of the Indians who were the legal
Possessors of that country. Crimes were
Commited that were a disgrace to civilization. Men
Were shot in cold blood, lands were confiscated.
Homes were burned and the inhabitants driven out

By these brigands. Chief Junaluska was personally
Acquainted with President Andrew Jackson.
Junaluska had taken five hundred of the flower of
His Cherokee scouts and helped Jackson to win the
Battle of the Horseshoe Bend, leaving thirty-three
Of them dead on the field. And in that battle
Junaluska had driven his tomahawk through the
Skull of a Creek warrior, when the Creek had
Jackson at his mercy. Chief John Russ sent
Junaluska as an envoy to plead with President
Jackson for protection for this, but Jackson's
Manner was cold and indifferent toward the rugged
Son of the forest who had saved his life. He met
Junaluska, heard his plea, but curtly said,
'Sir, your audience is ended, there is nothing I can
do for you.' The doom of the Cherokee was sealed.
Washington D.C. had decreed that they must be
Driven West, and their lands given to the White
Man, and in May 1838 an Army of four thousand
Regulars, and three thousand volunteers, under
Command of General Winfield Scott, marched into
The Indian country and wrote the blackest chapter
On the pages of our communal Amerikan History.
Men working in the fields were arrested and driven

To the stockades. Women were dragged from their
Homes by soldiers whose language they could not
Understand. Children were often separated from
Their parents and driven into the stockades with
The sky for a blanket and the earth for a pillow.
And often the old and the infirm were prodded
With bayonets to hasten them to the stockades.
In one home, death had come during the night, a
Little sad faced child had died and was lying
On a bear skin couch and some women were
Preparing the little boy for burial. All were
Arrested and driven out, leaving the child
In the cabin. I don't know who buried him.
In another home was a frail mother, apparently
A widow and three small children, one just a baby.
When told that she must go, the mother gathered
The children at her feet, prayed a humble prayer in
Their native tongue, patted the old family dog on
The head, told the faithful creature good-bye, with
A baby strapped on her back and leading a child
With each hand, started on her exile. But the task
Was too great for that frail mother. A stroke of
Heart failure relieved her sufferings. She sunk and
Died with her baby on her back, and her other two

Children clinging to her hands. Chief Junaluska,
Who had saved President Jackson's life at the battle
Of Horse Shoe Bend, witnessed this scene, the tears
Gushing down his cheeks and lifting his cap he
Turned his face toward the Heavens and said, 'Oh
My God, if I had known at the battle of the Horse
Shoe what I know now Amerikan History would
Have been differently written.' At this time, 1890,
We're too far from the removal of Cherokees for
Our young people to fully understand the enormity
Of the crime that was committed against a helpless
Race, truth is, the facts are being concealed from
The young people of today. School children of
Today do not know that we are living on lands that
Were taken from a helpless race at the bayonet
Point to satisfy the white man's greed for gold.
Future generations will read and condemn the act
And I do hope posterity will remember that private
Soldiers like myself, and like the four Cherokees
Who were forced by General Scott to shoot an
Indian Chief and his children, had to execute the
Orders of our superiors… We had no choice in the
Matter. Twenty-five years after the removal it was
My privilege to meet a large company of Cherokees

223

In uniform of the Confederate Army under
Command of Colonel Thomas, they were encamped
At Zollicoffer. I went to see them. Most of them
Were just boys at the time of the removal, but they
Instantly recognized me as 'the soldier that was
Good to us.' Being able to talk to them in their
Native language, I had an enjoyable day with them.
From them I learned that Chief John Ross was still
Ruler of the nation in 1863. And I wonder if he is
Still living. He was a noble hearted fellow, he
Suffered a lot for his race. His Christian wife
Sacrificed her life for a little girl who had
Pneumonia. The Anglo-Saxon race should build a
Towering monument to perpetuate her noble act in
Giving her only blanket for comfort of a sick child.
Incidentally, the child recovered, but Mrs. Ross is
Sleeping in an unmarked grave far from her Smoky
Mountain home. When Scott invaded the Indian
Country, some of the Cherokees fled to caves and
Dens in the mountains and were never captured and
They are there today. I have long intended going
There and trying to find them, but I have put off
Going from year to year and now I am too feeble to
Ride that far. The fleeting years have come and

Gone and old age has overtaken me.

I can say that neither my rifle, nor my knife are
Stained with Cherokee blood. I can truthfully say
That I did my best for them when they certainly did
Need a friend. Twenty-five years after the removal,
I still lived in their memory as 'the soldier who was
Good to us.' However, murder is murder, whether
Committed by the villain skulking in the dark or by
Uniformed men stepping to the strains of martial
Music. Murder is murder and somebody must
Answer, somebody must explain the streams of
Blood that flowed in the Indian country in the
Summer of 1838. Somebody must explain the four
Thousand silent graves that mark the trail of the
Cherokees to their exile. I wish I could forget it all,
But the picture of six hundred and forty-five
Wagons lumbering over the frozen ground with
Their cargo of suffering humanity still lingers in my
Memory. Let the Historian of a future day tell the
Sad story with its sighs and tears and dying groans,
Let the great Judge of all the earth weigh our
Actions and reward us according to our work. Thus
Ends my birthday story, this December 11th, 1890.

He blows out his birthday candles, letting them trail their lines of smoke up into the darkness. The smoke up into the air in curls and in lacy drifting's then is only, merely, more air.

SOME
HISTORICAL
SOURCES

B.A., Botkin . *A Treasury of American Folklore. 2.* Guilford: Globe Pequot, 2016. Print.

Burnett, John. *Cherokee Legends and the Trail of Tears.* Museum of the Cherokee Indian. Knoxville, TN. S.B. Newman Printing Company, 1956. Print.

Catharine Esther, Beecher and Harriet Beecher Stowe. *American Woman's Home.* Public Domain, 1869. Web.

David Brion, Davis and Steven Mintz. *The Boisterous Sea of Liberty. 2.* Oxford, New York: Oxford University Press, 1999. Print.

Dee, Brown. *Bury My Heart at Wounded Knee. 2.* New York: Henry Holt and Company , 2007. Print.

Frederick Jackson, Turner. *The Significance of the Frontier in American History.* Mansfield Centre: Martino Publishing, 2014. Print.

Richard, Erdoes and Alfonso Ortiz. *American Indian Myths and Legends.* New York: Pantheon Books, 1984. Print.

H.W., Brands. *Andrew Jackson: His Life and Times*. New York: Anchor Books, 2005. Print.

John W, Work. *American Negro Songs: 230 Folk Songs and Spirituals, Religious and Secular*. Mineola: Dover Publications, 1998. Print.

Jon, Meacham. *American Lion: Andrew Jackson in the White House*. New York: Random House Trade Paperbacks, 2009. Print.

Coming soon...

Joseph Eldredge's next book!

The Books of Amerika, Book III

AN ANTEBELLUM OZ

Will be available at

Choicepublications.com

Amazon,

Barnes & Noble,

Booksellers around the globe!